BUILDING EXPERT SYSTEMS:
Cognitive Emulation

ELLIS HORWOOD BOOKS IN INFORMATION TECHNOLOGY
General Editor: Dr. JOHN M. M. PINKERTON, Principal, McLean Pinkerton
Associates, Surrey, (formerly Manager of Strategic Requirements,
International Computers Limited)

STRATEGIC IMPLICATIONS AND APPLICATIONS OF EXPERT SYSTEMS
A. BEEREL, Director, Lysia Ltd., London

PRACTICAL MACHINE TRANSLATION
D. CLARKE and U. MAGNUSSON-MURRAY, Department of Applied Computing and
Mathematics, Cranfield Institute of Technology, Bedford

KNOWLEDGE-BASED EXPERT SYSTEMS IN INDUSTRY
J. KRIZ, Head of AI Group, Brown Boveri Research Center, Switzerland

ADVANCED INFORMATION TECHNOLOGY
J. M. M. PINKERTON, Principal, McLean Pinkerton, Esher

BUILDING EXPERT SYSTEMS: Cognitive Emulation
P. E. SLATTER, Product Designer, Telecomputing plc, Oxford

SPEECH AND LANGUAGE-BASED COMMUNICATION WITH MACHINES
J. A. WATERWORTH, British Telecom Research Laboratories, Ipswich

BUILDING EXPERT SYSTEMS:
Cognitive Emulation

P. E. SLATTER, Ph.D.
Product Designer
Telecomputing plc, Oxford

Special Adviser:
Professor J. Campbell
Department of Computer Science
University College London

ELLIS HORWOOD LIMITED
Publishers · Chichester

Halsted Press: a division of
JOHN WILEY & SONS
New York · Chichester · Brisbane · Toronto

First published in 1987 by
ELLIS HORWOOD LIMITED
Market Cross House, Cooper Street,
Chichester, West Sussex, PO19 1EB, England
The publisher's colophon is reproduced from James Gillison's drawing of the ancient Market Cross, Chichester.

Distributors:

Australia and New Zealand:
JACARANDA WILEY LIMITED
GPO Box 859, Brisbane, Queensland 4001, Australia

Canada:
JOHN WILEY & SONS CANADA LIMITED
22 Worcester Road, Rexdale, Ontario, Canada

Europe and Africa:
JOHN WILEY & SONS LIMITED
Baffins Lane, Chichester, West Sussex, England

North and South America and the rest of the world:
Halsted Press: a division of
JOHN WILEY & SONS
605 Third Avenue, New York, NY 10158, USA

© **1987 P.E. Slatter/Ellis Horwood Limited**

British Library Cataloguing in Publication Data
Slatter, P. E.
Building expert systems: cognitive emulation. —
(Ellis Horwood books in information technology).
1. Expert systems (Computer science)
I. Title
006.3'3   QA76.76.E95

Library of Congress Card No. 87–3760

ISBN 0–7458–0065–3 (Ellis Horwood Limited)
ISBN 0–470–20891–0 (Halsted Press)

Phototypeset in Times by Ellis Horwood Limited
Printed in Great Britain by R. J. Acford, Chichester

Contents

Preface

This book is primarily intended for *expert system practitioners* considering whether to adopt cognitive emulation as a fundamental design principle. More generally, it is intended for designers wishing to tackle the emulation issues that arise in expert system projects in a more informed way.

Considering also the emulation of human thinking in knowledge-based expert systems, it is, additionally an exploration of the interface between knowlege engineering and cognitive psychology. While the differences between expert system design and psychological modelling have occasionally been discussed, a detailed assessment of the viability and implications of a cognitive approach to knowledge engineering has yet to be carried out. The present book addresses this issue, and is also intended as an introduction to the subject.

The following groups of people might also find the book of use:

Cognitive psychologists looking to evaluate the relevance of their subject to the expert system field, and to compare and contrast existing cognitive models of human expertise with applied expert systems.

Others: those involved in the introduction of expert systems technology in commercial and industrial settings should find at least Chapters 1, 3 and 4 helpful. Finally, persons interested in the debate over the comparative nature of human and artificial intelligence may find that this book throws a revealing sidelight on that controversy.

The treatment of psychological issues in this book assumes no prior exposure to cognitive psychology. And while a familiarity with the basic concepts and terminology of the expert system field is assumed, a short Glossary of key terms is included to assist the more general reader. For introductory texts on expert systems Hayes-Roth *et al.* (1983) and Jackson (1986) can usefully be consulted. An extended introduction to modern cognitive psychology is provided in Anderson (1985).

This book has arisen from a research programme for a higher degree with the Open University. Over the last two years preliminary versions of parts of this book have appeared as a technical report, a conference paper, a review article (Slatter, 1985) and an Alvey Workshop paper (Slatter, 1986). Various individuals made valuable comments on these earlier efforts, and I would like to take this opportunity to collectively thank them. Some remarks by Ben du Boulay early on proved especially helpful. Thanks must also go to my supervisor at the Open University, Tim O'Shea. I am particularly indebted to John Fox, of the Imperial Cancer Research Fund, who acted as external supervisor in this research project. However, neither he, nor anyone else referred to, is responsible for the book's shortcomings — these are entirely attributable to the author. Finally, I would like to thank the chairman of Telecomputing plc, Bernard Panton, for making available the company's resources in producing this manuscript.

Philip Slatter

Oxford
January, 1987

1

Introduction

1.1 WHAT IS COGNITIVE EMULATION?

Expert systems use artificial intelligence (AI) techniques to solve problems ordinarily requiring human expertise. *Cognitive emulation* refers to a strategy in expert system design which seeks to emulate human thinking. A cognitive approach to knowledge engineering has several distinctive features:

(1) It attempts to embody in an expert system not just the human knowledge of a domain expert, but also the way an expert represents, utilizes and acquires that knowledge.
(2) The principle of cognitive emulation is usually defined to include the cognitive processes of system users, in addition to those of domain experts.
(3) It is explicit. It enables the issues of expert and user emulation that may arise during an expert system development to be tackled in an explicit and principled fashion.
(4) It attempts to emulate, using AI techniques, any aspect of human thinking that could assist in the construction of an expert system. This might include details of human memory organization, information processing limitations, problem solving and reasoning strategies, etc. It may also include emulation of the overall organization, or "architecture", of human cognition.
(5) It draws inspiration from empirical and theoretical investigations of human thinking — in particular, from research in Cognitive Psychology. The theories, hypotheses, computational models, methods and techniques of this branch of psychological science

are adapted for knowledge engineering purposes.

(6) It is a concern with the practicalities of knowledge engineering (e.g. computational efficiency, modifiability, usability), which principally distinguish cognitive emulation from the cognitive modelling of psychologists.

(7) At present, the influence of cognitive psychology on the expert systems field is essentially as depicted in Fig. 1.1, with the

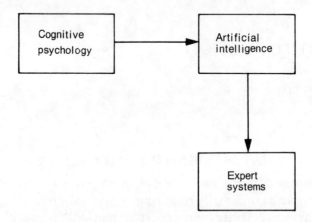

Fig. 1.1 — Existing indirect link between cognitive psychology and the expert systems field.

influence filtered through AI research. [AI scientists have capitalized on productive ideas derived from the study of human intelligence and developed them into a technology for creating artificial intelligence. Expert system designers employ this technology.] Adopting a cognitive approach implies supplementing this existing link with a more direct one, as shown in Fig. 1.2.

(8) Finally, 'cognitive emulation' is both a descriptive concept and a prescriptive principle. As a descriptive concept, it can be argued that most expert systems incorporate — albeit unintentionally — many features characteristic of human knowledge processing (see Section 3.1.1). As a prescriptive principle, 'cognitive emulation' refers to expert system work in which an explicit strategy of emulating human cognitive processes is followed. Furthermore, the attempt should be based on some testable method, technique or model — that is, not solely on the casual observations or intuitions of the designer. It is with this latter, prescriptive definition of 'cognitive emulation' that this book is primarily concerned.

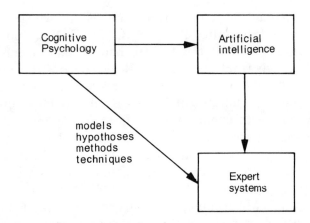

Fig. 1.2 — Additional direct link between cognitive psychology and the expert systems field implied by the cognitive emulation principle.

1.2 CURRENT STATUS OF THE EMULATION APPROACH

Throughout their brief history expert systems have been loosely modelled on the behaviour of human experts. However, systematic attempts at simulating experts' decision processes have only rarely been reported. Two early exceptions are: INTERNIST (Pople, 1982),which modelled the clinical reasoning of a diagnostician in internal medicine, and PSYCO (Fox, Barber and Bardhan, 1980), a system for diagnosing dyspepsia that incorporated various known principles of human information processing. The number of research projects involving a significant element of cognitive emulation has tended to increase in recent years (see, for example, papers in the volume edited by Coombs (1984) and Chapter 5 of this book). Similarly, the last few years have seen a growing awareness, among leading researchers, of the potential benefits of modelling human cognition more closely in expert systems(e.g. Clancey, 1984; Gaschnig *et al.*, 1983; Fox, 1982; Kuipers and Kassirer, 1984). Research is also underway to see how techniques developed in cognitive psychology can be used to facilitate knowledge acquisition from experts (e.g. Boose, 1984; Breuker and Wielinga, 1984; Gammack and Young, 1984).

However, despite this upsurge of interest, applications of the emulation principle in knowledge engineering are still the exception rather than the rule. Most of the best known systems — including MYCIN (Shortliffe, 1976), PROSPECTOR (Duda, Gaschnig and Hart, 1979), DENDRAL (Buchanan and Feigenbaum, 1978) and R1/XCON (McDermott, 1982) — were constructed with little or no explicit aim of modelling expert thinking. Outside of research-oriented establishments there is, if anything, even less explicit concern with cognitive emulation. In commercial applications of today's expert systems technology the emphasis is firmly on achieving expert–level performance using formal problem solving methods. This viewpoint is expressed in the technology-based definition of expert sytems offered by Johnson (1984, p.15) : "a set of computer programs which emulate human expertise by applying the techniques of *logical inference* to a knowledge base" (my italics).

One reason for the current status of the emulation strategy appears to be a general lack of appreciation among practitioners of the possibilities and issues associated with the emulation approach. But it could be argued that such an appreciation is not necessary. After all, if an explicit strategy of emulation is not a precondition of a successful expert system development — as systems such as DENDRAL and XCON appear to demonstrate — what justification can there be for adopting a cognitive approach? The pros and cons of emulation are dealt with in Chapters 3 and 4. For now, it is sufficient to point out that the objective of a well-articulated theory of knowledge engineering will only be achieved once all the relevant aspects of the subject — including cognitive emulation — have been properly evaluated. This book is intended as a contribution to this process of evaluation.

1.3   OBJECTIVES

This book is designed to perform a number of complementary roles:

(1) *Introductory text* It is intended to introduce the subject of cognitive emulation in a way that is accessible to the wider knowledge engineering community — not just to research workers familiar with this field.
(2) *Decision support* By making explicit the possibilities that exist for cognitive emulation, to help knowledge engineers make more informed decisions about adopting an explicit strategy of emulation in their own work. At the very least it should provide an informed basis for the handling of the emulation issues that can arise during an expert system development.
(3) *Feasibility study* To investigate the viability of a strategy of

cognitive emulation by exploring in detail the issues that arise when a cognitive approach to expert system design is attempted. This requires consideration of such questions as:

- how do human experts actually solve problems?
- is cognitive emulation a theoretical possibility?
- what factors are likely to facilitate and constrain a cognitive approach?
- how should one decide when an emulation approach is worth adopting?
- what are the different approaches to emulation that have been tried?

(4) *Information source* By supplying detailed references and an extensive bibliography of some 200 items, to provide the reader with the means to pursue particular lines of interest.

1.4 SCOPE

The scope of this book reflects these objectives:

First of all, the question of cognitive emulation is examined primarily from an (knowledge) "engineering" perspective. So, although the long-standing, and essentially philosophical, debate about the possibility of emulating human thinking in artificial systems is briefly referred to, this book is not directed to a further consideration of such meta-issues. Clearly, though, a book about cognitive emulation in expert systems is making a key assumption: namely, that in principle at least, computational models of human thinking are possible. Fortunately, this is an assumption shared by most workers in AI and cognitive science.

Second, this book is selective in which aspects of human cognition it deals with. Discussion focuses on cognitive processes relating to the "core" expert system topics of knowledge representation, knowledge acquisition, inferencing methods and system architecture. In the future, the human-like capabilities of expert systems are likely to be significantly enhanced by developments in such AI fields as natural language processing, vision and robotics. But these areas are not among the central concerns of knowledge engineers at present, and so are outside of the scope of this book.

The emulation principle is concerned with modelling human thinking in general, and the cognitive processes of selected categories of people in particular. Clearly, for the designers of computer systems intended to simulate expert-level performance, human experts are of primary interest. A whole chapter of this book is thus devoted to reviewing our present understanding of human expert thinking — as revealed by research in cognitive psychology. The other group to be singled out consists of the users of expert systems. It is now widely acknowledged that the acceptance of an expert system can critically depend on the system being designed in accordance with the expectations, knowledge and preferences of its intended users. However, questions of user emulation can arise with most kinds of interactive computer system — not just expert systems. So it is not surprising that the subject of user cognition and its emulation have long been of interest to researchers in human-computer interaction (see, for example, Hammond and Barnard, 1985). The discussion here is restricted to user emulation as it relates to expert system design.

In general, the subject of cognitive emulation in this book is dealt with at a conceptual rather than an a detailed implementational level. So, in discussing applications of the emulation principle, attention is centred on the ideas and concepts involved, the success or otherwise of the project, and any general problems encountered in implementing cognitive constructs. For details such as the programming techniques employed, the reader should consult the supplied references. Similarly, the results of research in cognitive psychology are presented in a condensed format. Such a presentation is necessary here — but at the risk of masking the true complexity of the psychological issues involved. Again, the interested reader should consult the supplied references to obtain a fuller analysis.

1.5   PREVIEW

The remainder of this book is organized as follows :

Chapter 2 reviews psychological research on human expert thinking. This provides a baseline for comparisons with machine expertise in subsequent chapters. To provide some background for those new to this area, the study of expert thinking is placed in the context of modern cognitive psychology. Next, the principal methods and techniques employed by psychologists examining expert cognition are examined. The remainder of the chapter is given over to a review of the published literature on the nature and development of human expertise.

Chapter 3 reviews the main arguments for and against cognitive emulation in expert system design. The tentative conclusion reached is that a significant degree of emulation is inevitable, but that a pure, unselective strategy of emulation is neither realistic nor desirable.

Chapter 4 examines the prospects for cognitive emulation from a more pragmatic angle. Several factors are identified that represent constraints on the usefulness of a cognitive approach. Special emphasis is given to detailing areas of conflict with other knowledge engineering objectives. However, a second set of factors is identified which should facilitate an emulation strategy — especially in the longer term. Some guidance is given on when to seriously consider adopting an emulation strategy.

Chapter 5 is the longest chapter. It presents a critical survey of expert system research that has already addressed the emulation issue. Six basic approaches to cognitive emulation are distinguished and evaluated. This helps draw out in more detail the implications of an emulation strategy for knowledge acquisition, knowledge representation and system architecture. The chapter concludes by discussing the issues that arise when different approaches to emulation are combined. Some guidance is offered on how this might be achieved.

Chapter 6, the last chapter, summarizes the main themes and issues to have emerged. This is followed by a summary of the design advice contained in the book.

2

Human expert thinking

2.1 INTRODUCTION

This chapter presents an overview of research on expert thinking and how it develops. The principal source is research in cognitive psychology. The chapter has three main objectives:

(1) *Appreciation.* It will indicate what a full commitment to a strategy of cognitive emulation in expert systems development could entail. This should provide an informed basis for the discussion of the emulation strategy in later chapters.
(2) *Heuristic.* It attempts to fulfil a heuristic role — showing how cognitive psychology can function as a useful source of ideas in expert system design.
(3) *Corrective.* It will aim to correct certain common misconceptions about the nature of expert thinking and what distinguishes it from novice thinking.

The following statements reflect some widely held beliefs about human expertise:

● Human expertise is acquired through experience.
● Human expertise is something mysterious and inexplicable.
● The superior performance of experts is based on superior intellectual ability.
● Experts reach conclusions by making a series of logical deductions based on the available evidence (Sherlock Holmes is a classic example from popular fiction of this view of the expert).

● The problem solving skill of physicists and engineers is attributable to "physical intuition".

A rather more subtle set of beliefs about human expertise —
based largely on casual observation, introspection, and the knowledge-based conception of human intelligence stemming from AI —
is apparent in the expert systems field. [The role of expert systems
development work as a stimulus to expertise research over the last
decade needs to be acknowledged. The knowledge engineering
enterprise has supplied cognitive psychology with new models of
expert thinking — not to mention a rationale for research funding.]
The collection below are all taken from the knowledge engineering
literature (e.g. Buchanan, 1982; Davis, 1982; Hayes-Roth, Waterman and Lenat, 1983):

● Expert performance depends on large amounts of domain
knowledge.
● Experts know when a problem is outside their area of competence, or when to break general rules in order to handle
exceptions.
● Experts can reorganize their knowledge into more appropriate
forms.
● Experts are capable of reflecting on their own cognitive processes
(meta-cognition), and know about their own state of domain
knowledge (meta-knowledge).
● Experts' reasoning and knowledge is frequently inaccessible.
● Expert cognition lacks both computational and representational
power.

As should become clear, most of these statements are broadly
consistent with cognitive research — after due elaboration and
refinement. [The main restriction in evaluating such assertions has
been the lack of coverage of certain topics in the psychological
literature. Given the differing concerns of knowledge engineers
and cognitive psychologists, however, such a mismatch is not
altogether surprising.]
The remainder of this chapter is organized as follows. Section
2.2 aims to place the study of human expertise in the context of
modern cognitive psychology. Section 2.3 comments on the principal methods and techniques adopted by psychologists interested
in expert thinking. Section 2.4 is the longest section: a review of
cognitive research on the many aspects of human expertise and its
development. Section 2.5 summarizes the picture of expert cogni-

tion to emerge from the preceding review. Finally, Section 2.6 provides some pointers to further reading.

2.2 COGNITIVE PSYCHOLOGY AND THE STUDY OF EXPERTISE

Cognitive psychology is currently the dominant approach within mainstream psychology. However it is still a young field, achieving a coherent identity only in the 1960s. Prior to this, Behaviourism — with its emphasis on observable behaviour and animal learning — significantly retarded research on human thinking over several decades: the notion of "mind" was anathema to Behaviourists. Cognitive psychology supplanted Behaviourism as the difficulties of explaining human behaviour without resort to such concepts as 'memory', 'imagery', 'reasoning', 'intelligence' and 'knowledge' became increasingly apparent.

Cognitive psychology is today a vigorously pursued subject employing scientific methods (see Section 2.3), but not yet with a coherent body of accepted theory. Many different theories, models and hypotheses are currently being explored, and some of the general principles underlying human thinking and performance are becoming clearer.

While there is not yet a coherent body of accepted theory, most cognitive psychologists adopt a common approach based on an *information processing* view of human cognition. An information processing system consists of a set of memories, receptors and affectors, and processes for acting on them (Simon, 1979). According to this approach, cognitive processes can be analysed into sequences of ordered stages. This entails identifying the sequence of mental operations through which information flows (and is transformed) in the performance of a particular cognitive task. Fig. 2.1 illustrates an information processing analysis of the stages involved in pattern recognition (it should not be taken too seriously).

Expert thinking is studied within this framework. The study of expertise has emerged as an identifiable area of psychological investigation only in the 1970s. Studies of changes in cognition from domain novice to domain expert — sometimes referred to as the "novice–expert shift" — now comprises a well-defined field within cognitive research. Indeed, one textbook on cognitive psychology (Anderson, 1985) devotes a separate chapter to the subject.

While expertise research represents an identifiable subfield, it is also heavily dependent on developments in other areas of cognitive

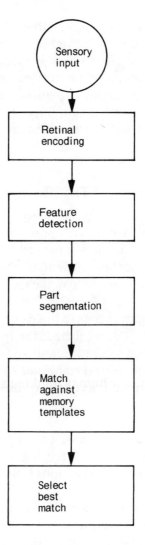

Fig. 2.1 — Illustrative information processing analysis of human visual perception.

psychology: i.e. research on memory, reasoning, problem solving, learning, etc.. This is because novice–expert differences are apparent in virtually all aspects of cognitive processing. Furthermore, it is becoming increasingly clear that the development of, on the one hand, specialist expertise, and, on the other, rather more mundane cognitive skills such as school arithmetic or driving a car, have many cognitive features in common (Anderson, 1985).

The close integration of expertise research with the rest of cognitive psychology implies that a satisfactory account of expert thinking will not be achieved independently of a general theory of human cognition. No attempt is made in this review to disguise the absence of a unifying theory, or indeed to develop one. As a consequence, conflicting explanations of key findings are sometimes presented. What we do attempt, however, is to identify the key elements of human expertise, and arrive at a coherent picture of how experts think.

2.3 METHODS AND TECHNIQUES

While this review is not primarily concerned with technical and methodological issues, an appreciation of the ways psychologists study expert cognition will nevertheless prove helpful. First, it will facilitate a proper assessment of the cognitive research reviewed below. Second, it may help make the technical literature a little more accessible.

Two main approaches to the study of novice-expert differences in cognition can be distinguished: the traditional psychological experiment, and a more recent "Cognitive Science" approach relying more on protocol analysis and computer simulation.

The main ingredients of the traditional psychological experiment are:

- Formulate a hypothesis (possibly an attempt to falsify some existing theory or to establish a new one).
- Deduce testable propositions from the theory — the experimental hypothesis.
- Assign subjects to control and experimental groups in an unbiased (e.g. random) fashion.
- Minimize the effects of all extraneous sources of variation and confounding variables.
- Systematically manipulate one or more independent variables and observe the effects on some measure of behaviour (called the dependent variable).
- Apply tests of statistical significance to results to see if they are properly attributable to the effects of "chance", or to the manipulation of the independent variable.
- Make an inference from the experimental findings to accept or reject the experimental hypothesis and the tested theory.

Doubts have been expressed about the appropriateness of a rigorous experimental approach to the study of human problem solving (e.g.

Card, Moran and Newell, 1983; Newell and Simon, 1972), and expert problem solving in particular (e.g. Larkin *et al.*, 1980). Criticisms include:

(1) Lack of ecological validity. The controlled/contrived situation of the typical psychological experiment can lead to a gross distortion of normal problem solving behaviour.
(2) An overemphasis on hypothesis-testing at the expense of quantitative measurements of cognitive processes.
(3) Standard experimental metrics such as reaction time are incommensurate with either the speed or richness of the cognitive processes underlying problem solving. For example, 15 minutes or more may elapse between the presentation of a problem statement to a laboratory subject and a solution being offered.

The limitations of a purely experimental approach are one reason for the emergence of an alternative approach in which protocol analysis and computer simulations of mental processes are the prime techniques. (This kind of research is sometimes called cognitive science.)

In expertise studies, protocol analysis involves making a verbatim recording of experts and novices as they "think aloud" during a problem solving exercise, and analysing the transcripts for similarities and differences. Verbal data obtained in this way provide a rich source of information about human thinking. The main limitations of this technique are:

(1) Verbal protocols, because they have to be interpreted, are not well suited to the objective quantitative comparisons required in formal hypothesis testing.
(2) Verbal protocols are often incomplete and inaccurate because of: the inaccessibility of "automated" knowledge (see Section 2.4.2(3)), interpreting rather than reporting by the subject, cognitive overload induced by the task, etc.. Problems with verbal data are dealt with in more detail in Section 5.2.
(3) Ambiguity. The results of a protocol analysis may be consistent with several distinct process models (Patel and Groen, 1986).

Protocol analysis is often used to provide the raw data for a computer simulation of cognitive processes under investigation. For example, a verbal protocol of a problem solving effort can be used to infer a set of production rules which, implemented as a production system, simulates the behaviour recorded in the protocol. Among the benefits claimed for cognitive modelling are:

(1) Modelling a psychological theory in a computer program intro-
    duces a requirement for explicitness and clarity into theory
    building that was not there before (Johnson-Laird and Wason,
    1977).
(2) It enables dynamic interactions between elements of a model to
    be studied and better understood by researchers (Slack, 1984).
(3) The need for explicitness and unexpected behaviour produced by
    the system can help generate new hypotheses (Slack, 1984).
(4) It gives credibility to a psychological explanation by showing that
    it is not dependent on vague mentalistic concepts, but instead can
    be operationalized in a working system (Larkin *et al.*, 1980).

Difficulties with computer simulations include:

(1) A lack of consensus in cognitive science as to the proper relation-
    ship between a program and the theory it seeks to embody
    (Slack, 1984). (An extreme position associated with Newell and
    Simon is to identify the program as the theory.)
(2) Ad hoc assumptions inserted into a program to ensure that it
    works can be hard to distinguish from the central theoretical
    ideas (Johnson-Laird and Wason, 1977).
(3) Published accounts of research do not necessarily correspond to
    any single working program (cf. Cendrowska and Bramer, 1984).

Virtually all the studies of expert thinking reviewed in this chapter
conform to either the traditional experimental approach (e.g. Adelson, 1984; Murphy and Wright, 1984), or the protocol/simulation
approach (e.g. Anderson, 1983b; Larkin *et al.*, 1980) or some
combination of the two (e.g. Chi, Feltovich and Glaser, 1981). The
two approaches are complementary rather than conflicting. For
example, experimental studies are well suited to testing hypotheses
about particular expert–novice differences, whereas computer simulation can be used to model the development from novice to expert.
Note that the methods and techniques just outlined have an obvious
bearing on the main theme of this book: Namely, the possibility of
cognitive emulation in expert system design. The methodological
issues surrounding the emulation strategy are dealt with more directly in Chapter 5.

    There is insufficient space in a review of this sort to give technical
details of all the studies cited. It is possible, however, to give some
indication of the range and variability of psychological research on
expertise.

(1) Subjects
In a typical experiment on expert cognition the main variable of interest is the level of expertise of the experimental subjects. The performance of groups of novices and experts on a cognitive task is compared. Occasionally subjects of intermediate expertise — "journeymen" — comprise a further experimental group (e.g. Murphy and Wright, 1984). Subjects are normally real specialists in some domain, but expertise is sometimes defined operationally; for example, in terms of how "knowledgeable" a subject is about a topic (c.f. Arkes and Freedman, 1984). The number of subjects involved can vary from one or two individuals studied intensively (Chase and Ericsson, 1982) to larger groups of around 50 (Adelson, 1984, Experiment 2), or even 100 or more (Tversky and Kahneman, 1983). Generally, studies in which protocol analysis and simulation are the central techniques rely on far fewer subjects than purely experimental studies (e.g. Anderson, 1983b).

(2) Domains
An impressive range of specialist skills have been studied:

- Chess (e.g. Chase and Simon, 1973; de Groot, 1965).
- Other boardgames such as Go and Gomoku (e.g. Eisenstadt and Kareev, 1975; Rayner, 1958).
- Mental calculation experts (Hunter, 1977).
- Medicine (e.g. Johnson et al., 1981; Kassirer and Gorry, 1978).
- Physics (e.g. Chi et al., 1981; Larkin, 1981).
- Algebra (Lewis, 1981) and geometry (Anderson, 1983b).
- Computer programming (e.g. Anderson, Farell and Sauers, 1984; Jeffries et al., 1981).
- etc.

(3) Tasks
In studies employing protocol analysis (e.g. Larkin et al., 1980), the primary task performed by novices and experts is usually an appropriate problem solving exercise; for example, simulated clinical diagnosis by medical practitioners. The secondary task is simultaneously giving the verbal protocol. In contrast, it is in the nature of experimental studies to focus on a single aspect of specialist expertise such as fact retrieval (e.g. Arkes and Freedman, 1984; Chase and Ericsson, 1982), devizing a suitable experimental task for the purpose. Conceptual sorting, attribute listing, sentence recognition, and reconstructing a chess position after a brief exposure to it, are representative of the cognitive tasks employed. The measures of

performance selected depend on the particular task. They include: error rates, comprehension time, number/size of sorted categories, eye movements, number of correctly repositioned chess pieces.

(4) *Treatment of results*

Experimental data of the sort just discussed are quantifiable, and hence amenable to tests of statistical significance. Analysed protocols yield more qualitative data, a popular use of which is in the building and testing of computer models of the development of expert cognition (e.g. Johnson *et al.*, 1981; Larkin *et al.*, 1980). Production systems have proved an especially popular formalism for implementing ideas about human expertise (e.g. Anderson, 1983b; Fox, Barber and Bardhan, 1980; Larkin, 1981) — although this may not imply a committment to production systems at the theoretical level (Young, 1979). Models of clinical expertise have made greater use of frame networks as a formalism (e.g. Pauker *et al.*,1976; Pople, 1982).

2.4   RESEARCH FINDINGS

Psychological research on expertise is reviewed here under the headings of Long-term Memory, Mental Operations and Working Memory. These headings correspond to the three basic architectural elements in contemporary models of both human information processing and expert systems (e.g. Card *et al.*, 1983; Hayes-Roth and Waterman, 1978): viz.

COGNITIVE ARCHITECTURE	EXPERT SYSTEM ARCHITECTURE
Working Memory (*or Short-Term Memory*)	Current Status Data Base (*or Dynamic Database*)
Long-term Memory (*or Permanent Memory*)	Knowledge Base (*or Static Data Base*)
Mental Operations (*or Cognitive Processor*)	Inference Engine (*or Interpreter*)

The material is organized in this way to emphasize the relevance of cognitive research on human expertise to knowledge engineering. For a detailed assessment of this model of the human cognitive architecture, and its relation to expert system architecture, see Section 5.6.2.

2.4.1   Long-term memory

An expert's store of permanent knowledge changes in various ways as they learn about a domain. Rumelhart and Norman (1978) distinguish three modes of change:

- *Accretion*. The accumulation of new knowledge within the framework set by existing memory structures.
- *Tuning*. Slight adaptations in existing memory structures to the naturally occurring variability of events in some domain.
- *Restructuring*. A major reorganization of memory structures prompted by inefficiency and over-complexity in the existing organization.

Accretion is a purely quantitative change, whereas tuning and restructuring are qualitative changes. Sections (1) and (2) below are included to illustrate the massive accretion of domain knowledge associated with becoming expert. In reality, though, the three types of learning tend to overlap — as sections (3) to (6) should make clear.

(1) *Facts*

Through attending lectures and seminars, reading textbooks and other formal channels, experts have accumulated a massive store of factual information that can be used in problem solving. The amounts involved are difficult to quantify, but appear huge. Consider for example the case of medical students, who may spend years studying and acquiring textbook knowledge about human physiology and diseases. Pauker *et al.* (1976) give a figure of between $\frac{1}{2}$ and 1 million as the number of core facts in general internal medicine alone — although there is no suggestion that the average intern will have acquired all this information! Similarly, Larkin *et al.* (1980) estimate that a single one-year course in American high school physics requires a student learning about 300 "things" — physics concepts and laws — from standard textbooks. Multiplied over several parallel courses and many years it is clear that prodigious quantities of factual knowledge must be acquired by many specialists.

(2) *Rules*

Quantitative estimates of expert knowledge are more often given in terms of the number of "rules" acquired than by the number of facts. Thus Simon and Gilmartin (1973) estimate that chess masters have learned in the order of 50 000 different chess patterns, i.e. recurring arrangements of pieces on the chess board. The recognition of such a pattern on the board is said to invoke stored knowledge about appropriate lines of action in that position. Production rules have frequently been used to model the development of expert skill as the acquisition of this kind of "pattern-action schemata" (Larkin *et al.*, 1980). Hence the rule measure of expertise. According to Hayes-Roth, 1985), to be expert in a profession requires at least 10 000 rules, with 100 000 rules representing the upper limit of human expertise.

(3) *Object categories*
Real-world objects can be perceived at several levels of abstraction: for example, the same item can be seen as a "piece of furniture", a "chair", a "kitchen chair", etc.. Human memory for object concepts appears to be organized in this kind of hierarchical fashion (Rosch *et al.*,1976). Rosch *et al.* suggest that experts are capable of making finer categorical distinctions than novices, and thus have more lower-level categories. Some research by Allan Whitfield and myself (Whitfield and Slatter, 1978, 1979) supports this suggestion. We found that whereas interior design experts identified Art Nouveau and Georgian as distinct furnishing styles, nonexpert subjects did not. Rather, the nonexperts judged exemplars of these two styles as belonging to a single "traditional" style category.

Together with this ability to make finer categorical discriminations, the expert is sensitive to more attributes of domain concepts (Murphy and Wright, 1984). This sensitivity can blur concept boundaries, however, as attributes previously associated with only one particular concept are recognized in exemplars of another concept, and vice versa. Usually when people learn a new concept they focus on the distinguishing features first. Thus, for example, training in medical diagnosis tends to start with classic textbook cases, before a more representative selection of case histories are encountered. As a consequence, experienced diagnosticians have concepts that are relatively *fuzzy*, in contrast to the more *crisp* concepts of the novice (Murphy and Wright, 1984). As single attributes become less predictive of category membership, experts may place geater emphasis on the predictive value of familiar *configurations* of attributes (see Section 2.4.1(5)).

Changes in conceptual organization are also likely as expertise develops (Murphy and Medin, 1985). New and more accurate interconnections between domain concepts are formed (e.g. Feltovich *et al.*, 1984). Moreover, even the correct concepts of novices may be organized differently. In one study (McKeithen *et al.*, 1981) novice programmers, when given the choice, chose to organize ALGOL reserved words alphabetically, whilst the experts favoured a semantic method of organization — grouping BEGIN with END, and so on.

(4) *Mental models*

In performing a complex task such as predicting the dynamic behaviour of a liquid, or using an interactive computer device, people access some kind of mental model (see, for example, the papers in Gentner and Stevens, 1983). Mental models help guide understanding and actions in dealing with artificial or natural systems. There is a lack of agreement at present among researchers as to the exact nature of mental models. A consensus position might be that mental models are more or less definite representations embodying structural and/or functional properties of the entity modelled.

Mental models appear to play an important role in expert problem solving. A study by Larkin (1983) compared how physics novices and experts modelled problems. Her findings suggest that novices have access only to a "naive" problem representation composed of objects that exist in the real world (e.g. pulleys, blocks). By contrast, the experts had access to an additional, "physical" representation containing imaginary entities such as momenta and forces. Thus the experts had developed a powerful second model which they could call upon. Other research has investigated expert circuit analysts' mental models of electronic circuits (de Kleer and Brown, 1983), the causal models of mechanisms of the human body employed by experienced physicians (Kuipers and Kassirer, 1984), and so on.

In summarizing this literature Forbus and Gentner (1986) make the following observations:

● In physical domains experts often acquire quantitative representations, e.g. mathematical models.
● Experts who have access to quantitative representations continue to update and use knowledge acquired at earlier stages of expertise acquisition, i.e. perceptual schemata, heuristic rules and qualitative models.
● Some domains, such as child-rearing, have no definitive models — forcing the expert to rely heavily on heuristic knowledge.

Another interesting point to emerge is that, unlike the elegant models found in textbooks, people's mental models tend to be deficient in various respects. That is, they are often messy, incomplete, and may include contradictory and erroneous concepts (Norman, 1983). However, through comparison with experiential knowledge gained on a relevant task, some debugging may take place (Williams, Hollan and Stevens, 1983).

To recapitulate: both novices and experts access mental models of entities in their subject domain. Experts' mental models are more accurate and domain-adapted, and they may have a larger range of models to choose from.

(5) *Indexing of knowledge*

Another cognitive correlate of the development of expertise is the ability to access knowledge rapidly as it becomes relevant to the present state of a problem solution. It can reach the point where access is almost instantaneous, and achieved with little or no conscious awareness (Larkin *et al.*, 1980).

This ability depends on the acquisition of a large number of perceptual patterns, or *chunks* (Miller, 1956), that directly index part of the expert's knowledge store. A chunk is a familiar configuration of elements that through repeated exposure comes to be recognized as a single unit. Chess research provides a good example: chess masters' ability to perceive a group of related chess pieces on a board is well documented (e.g. Chase and Simon, 1973). Similar chunking effects have been reported over an impressive range of expert domains (see Chase and Ericsson, 1982, for references).

With experience, experts learn to associate task-relevant knowledge with each pattern. Depending on the expert domain, the stored knowledge indexed can take a variety of forms; for example, appropriate lines of chess development (Chase and Simon, 1973, de Groot, 1965), physics principles (Larkin, 1981), facts relevant to programming design (Jeffries *et al.*, 1981), medical diagnostic categories (e.g. Szolovits and Pauker, 1978; Johnson *et al.*, 1981).

Cognitive scientists have modelled the development of indexing as the acquisition of production rules (e.g. Anderson, 1983b; Larkin, 1981). The condition part of the rule represents the indexing pattern which when "matched" evokes the attached action (knowledge). For instance, according to Larkin (1981), physics problem solvers gradually learn the conditions under which a particular principle is successfully applied, such that the appropriate principle is triggered automatically when the same conditions are detected again on a later occasion.

In conclusion: indexing reduces the need for an expert to solve a problem by exploring a large search space of possibilities. Rather, useful knowledge is retrieved from long-term memory at the time it is required.

(6) *Proceduralization of knowledge*
Declarative and procedural representations of knowledge can be distinguished (Winograd, 1975).

As expertise develops, there is a shift towards procedural forms of knowledge representation. For example, some evidence suggests that the arithmetic skills of school teachers are stored in memory as unanalysed procedures or "macros" (Brown and Burton, 1978). That is, while teachers are expert in performing arithmetic operations, they cannot readily verbalize what the operations are. Other research indicates that the declarative knowledge of problem solvers in physics (Chi *et al.*, 1981; Larkin *et al.*, 1980) and geometry (Anderson, 1983b) becomes increasingly proceduralized as expertise is acquired.

Anderson (1983a) presents a three stage theory of skill acquisition which aims to account for these changes. Briefly the stages are:

(a) DECLARATIVE STAGE Initially all new information is acquired in a declarative form; for example, facts from a text-book (modelled as the growing of semantic network structure). Declarative knowledge is interpreted by domain-independent problem solving procedures such as means–ends analysis.

(b) KNOWLEDGE COMPILATION STAGE In this stage the declarative knowledge is transformed into a procedural form (although the declarative representation may also be retained). The process is seen as analogous to the compiling of a computer program. Domain-specific procedures are acquired by recording the conditions under which a piece of declarative knowledge proves useful (modelled using production rules). Individual productions combine to form composite productions.

(c) PROCEDURAL STAGE In this stage procedures become more automated (see Section 2.4.2(2)) and faster. The ability to verbalize knowledge is lost. Procedures continue to be refined, or *tuned*. For example, *strengthening* process increases the probability of successful productions being invoked on a later occasion. Unsuccessful productions gradually fade in strength, but are never lost entirely.

In summary: the development of expertise involves the proceduralization of domain knowledge initially encoded in a declarative form. Through repeated use, these procedures are gradually refined and combined into large units.

2.4.2 Mental operations

(1) *Fact retrieval*

Experts are far better than novices at recalling facts about a domain (Arkes and Freedman, 1984). This robust finding presents a challenge to theories of memory that predict interference between facts during retrieval. That is, since experts know a massive number of facts about a domain, they ought to exhibit poorer memory than novices. The contrary is true however: experts generally retrieve domain knowledge with far greater speed and accuracy (e.g. Reder and Ross, 1983). This is the so-called "paradox of interference" (Smith, Adams and Schorr, 1978).

This phenomenon is open to a number of, not necessarily mutually exclusive, explanations:

(a) INDEXING Perceptual patterns in the current state of the problem solution automatically trigger the activation of relevant bits of knowledge. Indexing has already been discussed in Section 2.4.1(5).

(b) INTEGRATION With growing expertise associated facts become integrated into large knowledge units such as *scripts* (Smith *et al.*, 1978). (A script is a frame-like structure describing an appropriate sequence of events in a particular context). Smith *et al.* suggest that script facts are accessed as a unit, which would reduce the scope for interference dramatically. There is also plenty of evidence that in some domains (e.g. electronic circuitry, architecture) experts develop hierarchical structures for organizing their knowledge and are able to use these structures to facilitate recall (see Chase and Ericsson, 1982).

(c) EFFECTIVE ENCODING Skilled individuals may have learned to encode information such that when it is required in some context, the retrieval cues are sufficient to achieve recall (Chase and Ericsson, 1982; Jeffries *et al.*, 1981). Novices, on the other hand, often fail to retrieve knowledge in long-term memory that is relevant to the solution of some problem.

(d) PLAUSIBLE INFERENCE What experts may be doing in memory experiments is not so much recalling facts as inferring them. That is, experts seem able to make use of their extensive domain knowledge to infer what a correct or plausible response should be (Arkes and Freedman, 1984). Thus a chess master can make use of his knowledge of familiar positions to "reconstruct" the board after seeing it very briefly (Chase and Simon, 1973). More generally, people sometimes "recall" facts they have not encountered, but which are thematically related to facts they have encountered (Reder and Anderson, 1980).

To summarize: experts retrieve domain facts more quickly and accurately than novices. Several cognitive mechanisms may contribute to this superiority.

(2) *Automated and controlled cognitive processes*

The chess master's ability to play lightning chess against several opponents simultaneously illustrates an important component of expert skill — the automatization of cognitive processes with practice.

The distinction between *controlled* and *automated* mental processes (e.g. Shiffrin and Schneider, 1977) is now widely accepted within cognitive psychology. In sharp contrast with controlled processes (which are best exemplified by higher-level decisions and strategies), automated processes:

● are often parallel and independent in nature
● are unconstrained by working memory limitations
● run to completion automatically once initiated
● require considerable practice to develop, but are difficult to modify once learned
● are unavailable to introspection
● speed up gradually as the automated sequence is learned.

The last point is worth elaborating on, since it constitutes a very robust phenomenon. In fact the time needed to perform a cognitive task is consistently found to decrease as a log power function of practice on the task. This implies that performance will continue to benefit from practice, but by ever diminishing amounts (see e.g. Card, Moran and Newell, 1983). The benefits of speed up with practice are well illustrated in physics problem solving, where expert performance has been reported as four times faster than novice performance (Larkin *et al.*, 1980).

The above research indicates that some control processes are subject to automatization with practice. At the same time, experts appear to develop a flexible control over their reasoning processes at a high strategic level. For example:

● experts are often able to give a clear indication of how the main task is decomposed into sub-tasks, and of the temporal relationships between these sub-tasks (McDermott, 1982).
● like novices, experts can see when a particular strategy is failing, and "repair" or switch strategy accordingly in order to overcome

the impasse (Jansweiger *et al.*, 1986).
● experts are not necessarily restricted to a single, fixed strategy for performing a task. Rather, they seem able to adapt the way they decompose the task into sub-tasks, depending on the problem at hand (Wielinga and Breuker, 1986).

Newell and Rosenbloom (1981) propose a "chunking model" (see Section 2.4.1(5)) to explain speed up with practice. Assuming the time needed to perform a task depends on the number of knowledge chunks accessed, then skilled individuals — who have encoded their task knowledge in fewer, larger chunks — will perform the task faster.

The distinction between the automatization of cognitive skills and the proceduralization of knowledge (see Section 2.4.1 (6)) is probably more one of emphasis than of substance (Anderson, 1983a; Lesgold, 1984). Lesgold (1984) goes on to suggest that because of cognitive processing limits, complex skilled performance requires the prior proceduralization of component skills. Sternberg (1984) makes a similar point:

> ... complex verbal, mathematical, and other difficult tasks can feasibly be executed only because many of the operations involved in their performance have been automatized. Failure to automatize such operations, either fully or in part, results in a breakdown of information processing and hence less intelligent task performance. (p. 153)

To summarize: the cognitive skills of an expert become increasingly automatized with practice. Automatization can account for the greater speed and complexity of expert performance, but also for the inaccessibility of expert reasoning and task knowledge. (See next section.) While some processes become automated, experts are able to achieve flexible control over high-level strategic processes.

(3) *Accessibility of cognitive processes*
The cognitive changes reviewed so far have been essentially beneficial in their effects on expert performance. However, the well-documented inability of experts to verbalize about their cognitive processes (e.g. Welbank, 1983) is harder to view as a benefit — especially from the standpoint of the knowledge engineer.

Experts are not unique in having difficulty reporting on their own thinking, however. A review by Nisbett and Wilson (1977) concluded that people generally have little or no introspective access to higher order cognitive processes. Rather, Nisbett and Wilson argue that introspective reports are based on *a priori*, causal theories which plausibly explain how a particular stimulus leads to a particular response.

These conclusions have been qualified somewhat by later research. In particular, Ericsson and Simon (1980) reported findings indicating that a problem solver does have privileged access to what is at the *focus* of his or her attention at any moment; but is no better able to explain *shifts* of attention than an external observer. Furthermore, people are rarely able, when asked later, to give accurate reports on what they were thinking about during a problem solving exercise.

If, as it appears, people in general have only limited conscious access to their cognitive processes, the position of experts in this regard is more serious still. The main reason is the automatization of cognitive skills with practice (described in Section 2.4.2(2)), and the accompanying proceduralization of domain knowledge (Section 2.4.1(6)). The knowledge acquisition literature (e.g. Welbank, 1983) testifies to the difficulty experts have in articulating their domain knowledge and reasoning strategies.

Experimental research on this topic is scarce, although a study by Berry and Broadbent (1984) has considered the effects of several variables, including practice, on the ability of subjects to verbalize about their performance on a cognitive task. No increase in ability to verbalize about task knowledge with practice was found — indeed, there were some indications of a decrease in this ability.

In the absence of direct introspective access, experts may rely on *a priori* models of their own thinking of the kind suggested by Nisbett and Wilson (1977), and discussed above. Investigations of diagnostic reasoning by Kassirer and Gorry (1978), and others, supports this view. Clinicians often report that they use what amounts to a forward-chaining strategy, keeping many different hypotheses in mind (as prescribed in medical textbooks). In contrast, their observed behaviour suggests that they in fact employ a strategy more accurately described as "hypothesize-and-test"; i.e. they appeared to "guess" a particular hypothesis quickly, and then reason backwards to try to prove it.

In summary: people's awareness of their own mental processes is rather limited. The proceduralization of knowledge and automatization of cognitive skills that accompany the development of expertise, serve to make expert thinking even less accessible to introspection.

(4) *Mode of reasoning*

Characteristic differences exist in the reasoning styles of experts and novices in such domains as physics (Larkin, 1981; Larkin *et al.*, 1980) and geometry (Anderson, 1983b). The novices tend to *reason backwards*, whereas the experts tend to *reason forwards*.

The backward chaining approach of the novice appears to reflect their reliance on "weak" domain independent methods such as means-ends analysis (Larkin, 1981). To illustrate (from Larkin *et al.*, 1980, p.1338): when confronted with the problem of determining the velocity, v, of an object, the physics novice starts with this unknown. However, to determine v the acceleration, a, must first be determined. If a is also uninstantiated then an equation is found with a as the resultant; and so on, backward chaining until a set of equations is found from which a solution can be derived.

The cognitive load imposed by backward reasoning is heavy: managing goals and subgoals, storing and retrieving partially solved equations. Thus one advantage of the shift towards reasoning forward is that it greatly reduces this cognitive load in problem solving. The transition from backward to forward reasoning is gradual, and may depend on the indexing of knowledge described in Section 2.4.1(5). To reiterate briefly: when the novice is solving a problem in backward mode, and a bit of knowledge is found useful, the conditions under which it proved useful are stored; so that when on a later occasion similar conditions recur, the same bit of knowledge is automatically triggered. Forward chaining is effective only because the expert has learnt through experience which of the many alternative forward inferences are required for the final solution (Anderson, 1985).

Some other findings relevant to the relation of forward and backward reasoning include:

(a) Intermediate experts may start off using forward inferences, but complete a problem using backward chaining.
(b) Particularly awkward problems, or problems on the boundaries of the expert's domain, may require the expert to revert to a general problem solving strategy in order to solve them (Larkin *et al.*, 1980; Szolovits and Pauker, 1978).
(c) It is widely accepted in cognitive psychology that for any but the most rudimentary tasks, skilled human performance depends on a flexible intermixing of forward and backward reasoning (cf. automated and controlled processes).

It is important to realize that forward reasoning will develop only in domains where this is the most effective strategy. Physics and geometry are such domains — in each there is a rich set of "givens" which are more predictive of a solution than the goal statement is (Anderson, 1985).

This is not true of, say, computer programming, where the problem statement is richly predictive, whereas the "givens" of a particular programming language are not. Empirical studies of program design (Anderson, Farrell and Sauers, 1984; Jeffries *et al.*, 1981) have found instead that both experts and novices adopt what amounts to a backward chaining stategy: i.e. top-down program design. The interesting contrast noted in this domain is between the *depth-first* approach favoured by novices, compared to the *breadth-first* development strategy employed by the expert programmers. A breadth-first approach is advantageous because it enables the dependencies (and conflicts) among sub-goals to be detected at each design level before proceeding to the next.

Clinical diagnostic medicine is another domain with distinctive features and a characteristic reasoning style to match (e.g. Pauker *et al.*, 1976; Kassirer and Gorry, 1978). Among these features is the fact that a diagnosis can sometimes be confirmed or rejected only by performing particular clinical tests. Moreover, each test is relatively costly — in terms of money, time and risk to the patient. These tests must be weighed against each other to determine which tests, if any, to administer. It is also known that certain patterns of symptoms are imperfectly associated with certain diagnostic categories, and that experienced diagnosticians make use of these.

Such domain characteristics suggest the need for a strategy incorporating elements of backward chaining (test confirmation), uncertainty handling (test administering decisions, empirical disease-–symptom links), and forward inference (diagnostic hypotheses evoked by patterns of clinical data). The results of this domain analysis are consistent with the *hypothesize-and-test* strategy observed amongst clinical diagnosticians (Elstein, Shulman and Sprafka, 1978; Kassirer and Gorry, 1978). Typically, a pattern of clinical data might prompt a diagnostician to "guess" initially one or more hypotheses. These are then tested using backward chaining and taking into account the uncertainties involved. Clinicians employ various strategies to eliminate invalid hypotheses, and discriminate among others.

To summarize: Experts adopt reasoning strategies appropriate to the problem domain. They come to rely less on deductive reasoning and more on pattern recognition-based approaches.

(5) *Handling uncertainty*

In many expert domains decision making is characterized by an unavoidable element of uncertainty. Judgements are made about the likelihood of such uncertain events as the outcome of a medical test (see above) or the movement of share prices on the Stock Exchange. A line of research initiated by Kahneman and Tversky (see the collection of papers by Kahneman, Slovic and Tversky, 1982) has focused on comparing the uncertainty judgements of human subjects with outcomes based on statistical theory and the laws of probability. This research reveals that people are frequently insensitive to statistical variables such as sample size, correlation and base rate probabilities. Nor do people tend to analyse daily events into exhaustive lists of elementary possibilities (from which compound probabilities can be aggregated). Thus Bayes' Rule, and other well-established statistical techniques, have been effectively refuted as psychological hypotheses about everyday decision making.

Rather than grapple with the computational complexities demanded by formal methods, people appear to rely on a small set of heuristics — of which *representativeness* and *availability* are the best understood (Kahneman *et al.*, 1982).

Availability refers to the tendency of judging the likelihood of an event by how readily related information in memory can be retrieved. This can distort probability estimation as when someone overestimates the likelihood of being struck by lightning after reading a particularly vivid newspaper report on the subject.

Representativeness describes a human strategy for judgement under uncertainty where the likelihood of an item belonging to a particular class is based on how representative or typical an example of the class the item is. So, for example, a shy young woman might be judged more likely to be a librarian than a shop assistant, despite the fact that there are far more shop assistants than librarians in the population at large.

A training in statistics may insulate a person from making naive statistical errors such as the Gambler's Fallacy — the erroneous belief that, for example, the next in a series of coin tosses is more likely to be heads because the preceding few were all tails. However, experts are liable to the same biases in probabilistic judgement as laymen — especially in more subtle and complex cases (Kahneman *et al.*, 1982; Tversky and Kahneman, 1983). This is not to deny that a statistical training can increase the likelihood of someone adopting a statistical approach, and producing a better solution as a result; but even where this is the case, it may have more to do with adherence to subcultural norms within a professional group, than to a greater appreciation of variability and uncertainty within a domain (Nisbett *et al.*, 1983).

The confidence an expert expresses in his or her own beliefs appears to depend on more than just representativeness and availability:

(a) *Redundancy of knowledge* The greater the redundancy of stored information about an event the greater the certainty in judgements relating to that event (Chase and Ericsson, 1982).

(b) *Lack-of-knowledge inference* This is a meta-inference based on knowledge about one's own knowledge, in which the absence of knowledge relating to an hypothesis is taken as evidence that an assertion is false. There is evidence that experts may place greater reliance than novices on this meta-inference (Gentner and Collins, 1981).

(c) *Self-generated stimuli* Experts, but not novices, are capable of inferring the presence of non-existent stimuli (see Arkes and Freedman, 1984). It was noted in Section 2.4.1(5) that the development of expertise is often accompanied by an integration of isolated facts into schemata. Schematic knowledge undergoes dynamic changes and distortions in memory (e.g. Bartlett 1932; Schank, 1982) — changes that tend to exaggerate distinctive features and "smooth out" unremarkable features in line with stored prototypes. This account goes some way to explaining why, for example, a clinician might "remember" that a patient was suffering from non-existent symptoms, should those symptoms confirm an earlier diagnosis; and "the rampant overconfidence of experts in many real-world judgement tasks" (Arkes and Freedman, 1984, p.439).

The research reviewed so far suggests that human (expert) judgement of uncertain events invariably compares unfavourably with formal statistical approaches. This impression needs to be qualified somewhat. While it is true that human experts are generally rather poor at making *quantitative* judgements, they appear far more successful when it comes to the *qualitative* handling of uncertainty. The following examples are from Zimmer (1984): livestock judges are able to handle up to ten variables simultaneously; it has been found that where data is highly configural, subjective judgement can be better than statistical prediction; exchange rate prediction by German bank clerks was more accurate where forecasts were made verbally rather than numerically. Further, a computer simulation of clinical reasoning by Fox *et al.* (1980) found that a nonprobabilistic approach involving pattern-matching on configurations of medical symptoms, produced diagnostic results comparable with results derived from a Bayesian statistical model.

To summarize: In making quantitative estimates about uncertain events, experts and laymen tend to rely on heuristic strategies such as Availability rather than computationally demanding statistical rules. Within a domain, experts appear better at making qualitative assessments, since these appear to rely heavily on learned configurations and pattern recognition.

2.4.3 Working memory
(1) *Working memory capacity*
Experts have larger memories for domain knowledge than novices.

Cognitive psychologists have long considered the capacity of working memory as a major bottleneck in human thinking. Its restricted capacity imposes a fundamental limitation on people's ability to think, reason and process information generally (e.g. Johnson-Laird, 1982; Miller, 1956; Newell and Simon, 1972). While a consensus as to the precise nature of working memory has yet to emerge (Chase and Ericsson, 1982), there is general agreement that its capacity is no more than about seven unrelated symbols.

However, as Miller (1956) pointed out, each symbol comprises a meaningful *chunk* (see Section 2.4.1(5)). This allows for considerable variation in the amount of actual information held in working memory, depending on chunk size. In particular, experts' chunks tend to be larger than novices. The classic demonstration of this comes from chess research (Chase and Simon, 1973; de Groot, 1965). In these experiments the task was to reconstruct a chess middle game position of some 25 pieces after viewing it for a few seconds. Chess masters were able to reconstruct the board position with about 90 percent accuracy. Novice players, on the other hand, struggled to replace more than 5 or 6 pieces correctly. The chess master's superior performance is based on an ability to process familiar configurations of pieces as single chunks; for the weak player each separate piece is a chunk. Thus when the task is repeated with a completely scrambled board postion — containing no meaningful configurations — experts perform no better than novices. Analogues of this experiment in many other domains have produced comparable results (see Chase and Ericsson, 1982, for references).

Chunking is not the only mechanism accounting for the larger working memory of the expert. As cognitive processes become automatized (see Section 2.4.2(2)) they make less demands on working memory capacity, which in turn leaves more space available for information storage. This can explain why skilled readers have expanded working memories for what they read, but not for information in general (Daneman and Carpenter, 1980).

Chase and Ericsson (1982) found a dramatic speed up in encoding and retrieval operations for information in long-term memory with high levels of practice (hundreds of hours). At these levels of skill, retrieval times from long-term memory come to approach those from working memory. The result is that the *effective* size of working memory can exceed normal capacity many times over. Chase and Ericsson (1982) claim this extra workspace as one reason why expert performance is superior to that of novices in so many domains.

In summary: the expanded working memory of experts is domain-specific. It is attributable to factors associated with practice — chunking, automatization and directly retrievable long-term information.

(2) *Problem formulation*

How a problem initially gets represented is crucial in determining how, and even if, it eventually gets solved (a point that emerges clearly from the AI literature). It is therefore worth considering the different ways experts and novices formulate problems.

One difference is in the time spent in arriving at a working representation of the problem. There is evidence that experts in such domains as physics (e.g. Larkin *et al.*, 1980), political science (see Lesgold, 1984, p.35) and computer programming (e.g. Jeffries *et al.*, 1981) take longer than novices in formulating a problem. This investment in attempting to understand the problem fully before proceeding is rewarded by a faster solution time overall, and an increased likelihood of achieving a correct solution. [The longer length of time experts take in problem formulation is the main exception to the earlier claim that expert processing is faster than novices (Section 2.4.2(2)). Experts nevertheless obtain their solutions more quickly overall.]

A second important difference concerns the relative *abstractness* of the problem representations. Research on the novice–expert shift in algebra (Lewis, 1981), chess (e.g. Chase and Simon, 1973), computer program design (Adelson, 1984) and physics (Chi *et al.*, 1981) indicates that the working representations used by experts are in general more abstract than those employed by novices. This expresses itself in different ways in different domains. For example,

Chi *et al.* (1981) found that physics novices represented problems in terms of features contained explicitly in the problem statement (e.g. falling bodies); whereas the experts categorized problems by the major physics principle used in the solution (e.g. the conservation of energy). In the domain of computer programming, the distinction is between representations reflecting what a program does (experts), as against how a program functions (novices) (Adelson, 1984).

The shift from concrete to abstract ways of representing problems depends on acquiring a new set of concepts for the purpose. With regard to programming, this means new concepts to support language-independent representations of problems (Anderson, 1985).

One advantage of abstract representations is that they hide detail, and thus allow more complex problems to be accommodated within the limited capacity of working memory. In the case of algebra, for example, a complex mathematical expression may be replaced by a single variable (Lewis, 1981).

A further advantage is that experts should be better able to reason by analogy — since abstract coding facilitates the analogical transfer of knowledge from one domain to another (Gick and Holyoak, 1983). Moreover, as experience in a domain increases, the basis of similarity matches shifts from massive feature overlap and surface-oriented matches, to matches based on fewer, but more abstract features (Forbus and Gentner, 1986).

What are the stages involved in formulating working representations of problems? Chi *et al.* (1981) present an account that stresses the role of problem *categorization* in the formulation process of physics experts:

- extract surface features directly from statement of problem
- derive abstract features from surface features using domain knowledge
- categorize problem according to solution principle involved, using derived features
- verify categorization using tests specified by the category ("schema")
- use knowledge in schema to complete formulation of problem

(At least step 2 is not applicable to novices.) The completed representation supports a forward reasoning solution method (Chi *et al.*, 1981). Larkin's (1983) account is similar. Physics experts select from memory a general schema embodying a relevant physics principle (e.g. a forces schema). A working representation is then constructed by instantiating the schema slots. Bhaskar and Simon (1977) also adduced evidence for the role of stored problem templates in expert problem formulation.

To recapitulate: experts take longer than novices to achieve an initial representation for a problem. Experts' working representations are more abstract and solution-oriented, and may depend on access to indexed problem schemata.

2.5   SUMMARY AND CONCLUSIONS

This chapter has reviewed psychological research on the development of expert thinking. Many facets of cognition change as expertise is acquired. Table 2.1 summarizes the principal changes covered in this review, classifying them as either "benefits" or "costs" depending on their impact on expert performance. From the table it is clear that the changes are predominantly beneficial.

One important point to emerge is that the cognitive correlates of expertise, whether beneficial or otherwise, are essentially *domain-specific* in effect. Thus outside his or her specialist area any cognitive advantage the expert may have enjoyed inside the domain quickly disappears.

It is also possible to say that an expert's thinking becomes increasingly *domain-adapted*. That is, many aspects of expert thinking get progressively more tailored to the unique characteristics of a particular domain. We examined the tendency to domain-adaptivity with regard to changes in reasoning style (2.4.2(4)) in particular. But it applies equally to, say, the development of appropriate mental models (2.4.1(4)) and working representations of problems (2.4.3(2)).

Another underlying theme in the development of expertise is a greater reliance on pattern recognition and memory (stored knowledge) at the expense of deductive reasoning. Indeed, at one level acquiring expertise can be seen as an adapting to the "natural" processing mode of the human brain — which has often been characterized as a highly parallel, pattern-oriented system (e.g. Anderson, 1983a). At another level, though, experts often show an impressive ability to reflect on, and flexibly control, their high-level task strategies. But precisely how automated skills and control strategies combine in expert problem solving remains poorly understood.

A review of this sort can only hint at the subtlety and complexity of human cognition in general, and expert cognition in particular. For example, little has been said about individual variation in how

Table 2.1 — Cognitive changes with expertise classified as benefits and costs

Change	Section
BENEFITS	
Increase in quantity of domain knowledge:	
facts	2.4.1(1)
rules	2.4.1(2)
concepts	2.4.1(3)
Refinement of domain knowledge:	
fuzzier categories	2.4.1(3)
debugged mental models	2.4.1(4)
Development of specialized representations:	
mental models	2.4.1(4)
Integration of domain knowledge:	
chunking	2.4.1(5)
schemata	2.4.2(1)
hierarchies	2.4.2(1)
cross-referencing	2.4.1(3)
composite procedures	2.4.1(6)
More efficient fact retrieval	2.4.2(1)
More flexible control over task strategies	2.4.2(2)
Speed up and tuning of cognitive skills	2.4.2(2)
Development of domain-specific reasoning strategies	2.4.2(4)
Improved qualitative handling of uncertainty	2.4.2(5)
Enhanced working memory capacity	2.4.3(1)
More solution-oriented problem representation	2.4.3(2)
More abstract coding of knowledge	2.4.3(2)
COSTS	
Reduced ability to report on cognitive processes	2.4.2(3)
Inaccessibility of proceduralized task knowledge	2.4.2(3)
Overconfidence in quantitative judgement	2.4.2(5)

experts think. This is mainly because in psychological studies of expertise the principle comparison of interest is between various groups of subjects: usually experts and novices. Expert differences have received more attention in the knowledge engineering field, as we shall see later. The present chapter has focused instead on what is distinctive in expert thinking. As the theme of cognitive emulation in expert system design is elaborated on in subsequent chapters, there will be cause to examine aspects of human cognition not yet considered.

2.6 SUGGESTED READING

Lesgold (1984) and Anderson (1985, Chapter 9) both review the literature on expert thinking. They should be consulted for an alternative perspective. Anderson (1985) is also a readable and up-to-date textbook on cognitive psychology in general. The book by Card, Moran and Newell (1983) provides a good introduction to applied cognitive psychology for those familiar with interactive computing. These authors present a simplified model of human information processing for the purposes of designing effective human–computer interfaces. Breuker and Wielinga (1983a) and Welbank (1983) discuss psychological research as it relates to knowledge acquisition from human experts. For an integrated theoretical account of the development of expertise see Kolodner (1984).

Papers on expert cognition are carried by a large variety of technical journals (see references to this chapter), including *Cognitive Science*, *Cognitive Psychology* and *The International Journal of Man-Machine Studies*. Much of the literature on clinical expertise is to be found in medical journals. A good collection of papers to start on are those by Chase and Simon (1973), Chi *et al.* (1981), Larkin *et al.* (1980) and Chase and Ericsson (1982). Finally, the references to this chapter should be consulted for further information on specific topics of interest to the reader.

3

Arguments for and against emulation

This chapter reviews the main arguments for and against the principle of cognitive emulation. Consideration of other, more pragmatic issues is reserved until the next chapter.

3.1 ARGUMENTS FOR COGNITIVE EMULATION

3.1.1 Cognitive emulation is inherent in knowledge engineering

As presently conceived expert systems almost inevitably approximate human expert thinking to a significant degree. This is because expert systems make use of domain knowledge ordinarily elicited from a human expert for solving problems. Indeed, knowledge-based techniques are a defining characteristic of the current generation of expert systems. Cognitive research clearly shows how dependent human expert performance is on the use of large quantities of specialist knowledge acquired over many years (see Chapter 2).

Knowledge-based approaches have evolved for sound pragmatic reasons and should thus endure. Initially, AI researchers sought to solve problems normally requiring human expertise using formal, domain-independent methods. It was the ineffectiveness of such methods, coupled with the subsequent success of experimental systems employing domain knowledge, that has led to the present emphasis on knowledge-based techniques. The history of the DEN-DRAL project (Buchanan and Feigenbaum, 1978), clearly illustrates this change.

Many expert system builders would go further and argue that it is necessary to capture something of how the expert *represents* his or her knowledge, and the reasoning strategies employed, in order to construct an effective system (Welbank, 1983).

Rule-based approaches, and in particular production systems, can be seen in this light. Rule-based formalisms are currently the most popular approach to knowledge representation, and the term "expert system" is sometimes formally defined as using rule-based techniques (Simons, 1983, p.115). Psychological validity has been claimed for this formalism by expert system researchers (e.g. Leith, 1983), reference usually being made to Newell and Simon's (1972) pioneering use of production systems for simulating human problem solving. Subsequently, production systems have been employed in modelling a variety of cognitive processes (Young, 1979). Anderson's (1976, 1983a) ACT represents an ambitious attempt to model human cognition using an architecture based on production systems. Regarding "rules" generally, there is a large volume of psychological research indicating that *certain* types of expert knowledge may be mentally represented in a rule-like form, i.e. empirical associations, pattern-indexed schemata, procedural knowledge, etc. (see Chapter 2). Despite these clear claims to psychological plausibility it is clear that rule-based formalisms have evolved as a major technique principally because of their knowledge engineering virtues (e.g. modularity) (Barr and Feigenbaum, 1981; Davis and King, 1977).

Other knowledge representation formalisms are supported by commercially available expert system packages (Hayes-Roth, Waterman and Lenat, 1983) For example, frames and semantic networks. As with production systems, these formalisms are taken very seriously as psychological models (e.g. Anderson, 1976; Anderson and Bower, 1973; Minsky, 1975).

An equivalent point can be made about inferencing methods. A deep analysis of expert systems indicates that they typically solve problems by the method of "heuristic classification" (Clancey, 1985). [Briefly, this method relates a specific problem to a specific solution in three steps, by : (1) *abstraction* from case-specific data to a general problem class ; (2) an *heuristic match*, based on experience, from the problem class to a solution class; and (3) *refinement* of the solution class to yield a case-specific solution.] This inference structure is found to correspond closely to psychological models of expert problem solving (see Clancey, 1985).

The use of machine induction techniques to produce a knowledge base does not represent an exception to the inevitability of cognitive emulation in knowledge engineering. This is because a domain specialist's knowledge is usually employed in the initial selection of concepts, attributes and exemplars. Consequently, these selections will reflect the experts' underlying conceptualization of the domain.

Moreover, atleast one well-known machine induction product — Donald Michie's Expert Ease — is derived from an algorithm originating in psychological research : Hunt's Concept Learning System (Hunt, Marin and Stone, 1966).

Breuker and Wielinga (1983a) effectively encapsulate the present argument when they observe (p. 24):

> In general there is a large overlap between knowledge-based systems and psychological models of the same task for the simple reason that up to now it is hard to conceive of more general, intelligent methods than those used by human(expert)s.

3.1.2 Cognitive emulation offers a principled approach to design

Probability theory, predicate logic and other formal methods are problem solving techniques founded on established mathematical and logical principles. This helps explain the attractiveness of such techniques to many expert system practitioners. Research is also under way (e.g. Fox, 1984a, 1984b) towards formulating a knowledge-based theory of decision-making comparable in rigour to statistical decision theory, but relying more on qualitative rather than quantitative techniques. While this work is informed by a concern for human intelligibility and fidelity to human modes of reasoning, it also aims at integrating knowledge-based and formal methods where this seems appropriate.

However, even without the buttressing of formal methods, cognitive emulation can offer a principled approach to knowledge engineering. In cognitive modelling exercises (see e.g. Hayes-Roth, Waterman and Lenat, 1978; Young, 1979) the known or presumed characteristics of human information processing are translated into a set of simplicity and purity constraints on program design. In production systems used as simulation programs this can take the form of self-imposed limitations on rule size and complexity, condition-driven control, uniformity in the rule base, etc. The main problem with such a purist approach is the loss of computational power that often results. While this may even be an advantage in cognitive modelling (Young, 1979), in applied expert systems it is usually unacceptable.

To avoid such conflicts, the emulation principle may be invoked more selectively (Fox, 1982). This would results in a correspondingly less principled approach to design, but one which remains informed by a unifying conception — human cognition.

3.1.3 Performance

Expert systems seek to achieve expert-level performance. Often the only available criterion for assessing the effectiveness of a built system is to compare its behaviour with that of one or more human experts — the so-called "gold standard" (Hayes-Roth, Waterman and Lenat, 1983). In the absence of more objective criteria, a plausible strategy for achieving expert-level performance is thus to model the underlying (cognitive) processes. The view of Gaschnig *et al.* (1983, p. 255) is relevant here:

> There is increasing realisation that expert-level performance may require heightened attention to the mechanisms by which domain experts actually solve the problems for which the expert systems are typically built. It is with regard to this issue that the interface between knowledge engineering and cognitive psychology is the greatest.

3.1.4 User acceptance

Gaining acceptance for a built system is now a major consideration in expert system design (Duda and Shortliffe, 1983; Hayes-Roth *et al.*, 1983). This stems from the failure of such famous expert systems as MYCIN to be accepted in daily use by the intended users, leading to the realisation that the achievement of expert-level performance *per se* is insufficient to guarantee user acceptance. In so far as it leads to greater intelligibility in the system's knowledge and the processes using it, and to a greater tolerance of intervention by the user, cognitive emulation can be expected to promote user acceptance (Aikins, 1983, p.199; Fox, 1982).

In addition, the "cognitive coupling" (Woods, 1986) between user and system also has implications for user acceptance. Earlier expert systems were often technology-driven problem solvers, with the user's role merely that of data gathering and filtering out poor system solutions. Users have tended to reject such a passive role (Coombs and Alty, 1984). Recent research is directed to supporting a far wider range of cognitive functions (see Section 5.4), with acceptability a major criterion.

A related argument is that cognitive emulation is morally or socially desirable: it could help humanize what might otherwise become an alien, machine-oriented technology (e.g. Fox, 1983; Michie, 1980).

3.1.5   More effective knowledge acquisition and representation
Building any non-trivial expert system is a difficult and time-consuming process. It has recently been argued that a major contributory factor is the inappropriateness of techniques currently used by system builders to both elicit and represent experts' knowledge (Gammack and Young, 1984; Young, 1985). Even within a narrow domain an expert's knowledge can be of many different types; much of it difficult to capture and express as empirical rules. It is thus possible to argue for the use of a variety of psychologically orientated techniques in both knowledge elicitation and knowledge representation. For example, Wilkins, Buchanan and Clancey (1984) have advocated modelling the expert's knowledge acquisition and knowledge organization methods in order to facilitate system development. (See Chapter 5.)

3.2   ARGUMENTS AGAINST COGNITIVE EMULATION

3.2.1   Human cognitive weakness
Human cognition compares unfavourably with computer systems in a number of respects:

- Human memory is prone to forgetting and distortion of stored information (Baddeley, 1976; Bartlett, 1932).
- The rationality of human thinking (in the formal logical sense) can be questioned. Certainly, aspects of deductive reasoning such as negation prove highly problematical for human subjects (Johnson-Laird, 1982; Johnson-Laird and Wason, 1977).
- People experience difficulties with probabilities, especially in handling combinations of uncertain evidence (Kahneman, Slovic and Tversky, 1982).
- Human information processing capacity is severely limited (Miller, 1956).

Put another way, computer systems already outstrip human capabilities in tasks such as arithmetic, rote memory and the application of standard problem-solving procedures; and they now perform comparably well in such areas as chess and text recognition (Sowa, 1984).

While it is valid to make these observations about the comparative weaknesses of human thinking, any conclusion regarding the superiority of formal computer systems needs strong qualification. First, people are able to employ a wide variety of "heuristics" and other knowledge-based capabilities, which may effectively compensate for a lack of computational power (Anderson, 1983a; Kahneman *et al.*, 1982). Moreover, for many interesting problems in AI all the known algorithms take an exponential amount of time; whereas practical heuristics derived from observing human performance can produce adequate solutions in reasonable amounts of time (Sowa, 1984). Second, the difficulty people experience with memory retrieval does not imply that computer-based storage systems are superior. That is to say, human memory — despite problems of forgetting, distortion, etc. — appears better adapted than existing computer systems to maintaining a huge data base of millions of facts, whilst enabling rapid access to all its knowledge (Anderson, 1984).

To conclude: The greater power and accuracy of formal computer systems argues against an unselective strategy of cognitive emulation. However, it does not provide a conclusive argument against a more selective strategy, because human cognition has compensatory strengths.

3.2.2   Inefficient and suboptimal representations

It can be argued that people make suboptimal decisions because they are incapable of using certain types of (optimal) representations of problems. This assertion has yet to be demonstrated, however (Fox, 1982). Neither has it been shown that computer programs can invariably support more satisfactory problem representations.

A related, and more plausible argument is that computer programs can represent an expert's knowledge in a highly compact form; certainly more efficiently than a human expert is capable. A familiar knowledge engineering practice is to elicit knowledge from an expert in modular chunks (facts, rules, etc.), and at a later stage compile these into a more efficient representation such as a decision tree or network. This has led some researchers to opt for efficiency rather than fidelity to an expert's representation in expert systems design (Welbank, 1983). They recommend translation to and from a more natural representation purely for the user's benefit.

3.2.3   Improving on expert performance

Human experts are known to be inconsistent, unreliable and to disagree with their colleagues on important matters (Gaschnig *et al.*, 1983; Welbank, 1983). Such observations suggest that a reasonable goal for expert system design is not merely the achievement of expert level performance but, ultimately, an improvement on human expertise. Results presented by Michalski and Chilausky (1980), where machine-induced rules proved better at diagnosing soybean diseases than rules derived from an expert, indicate that this is already the case for some simple types of task. And logically, it is difficult to see how the objective of improving on human performance could be achieved in an expert system modelled purely on an expert's thinking, weaknesses as well as strengths.

3.2.4   Multiple expert systems

In knowledge engineering there is often a requirement to embody the expertise of specialists from different areas within a single expert program. This requirement is reflected in the commercially available "blackboard" architecture for expert systems. [Problem-solving in a blackboard system involves a set of independent "specialists" or knowledge sources co-operating in developing and testing possible solutions. Communication is via a shared working memory: the blackboard.] Even in the more general case — where only the expertise of one particular type of domain specialist is at issue — it is considered that to be useful an expert system should be capable of embodying the expert skill of several individuals (Welbank, 1983).

This "multiple expert" feature constitutes an argument against cognitive emulation in its strongest form. That is to say, whilst general principles underlying human thinking are discernible, the cognitive processes of different individuals cannot be combined or averaged very meaningfully. Not least this is because individual variation is such a salient characteristic of human cognition (see e.g. Newell and Simon, 1972). Even within a particular specialty different experts can be expected to employ idiosyncratic reasoning strategies and knowledge representations (Kuipers and Kassirer, 1984).

3.3   CONCLUSIONS

This chapter has presented the major arguments for and against cognitive emulation as an expert system design strategy. Taken together the force of these arguments is that neither extreme attitude to cognitive emulation is tenable.

Thus, on the one hand, a pure, unselective application of the strategy is untenable because:

● it would entail a commitment to emulating human cognitive weakness (3.2.1)
● experts' representations of problems may be sub-optimal or inefficient (3.2.2)
● it implies that expert systems cannot aim to improve on human expert performance (3.2.3)
● some expert systems require the expertise of several domain specialists (3.2.4)

Equally, the opposite view that cognitive emulation should be avoided or ignored as a design strategy can also be discounted since:

- cognitive emulation seems inherent in knowledge engineering (3.1.1)
- cognitive emulation offers a principled approach to expert system design (3.1.2)
- a plausible strategy for achieving expert-level performance is to emulate the underlying cognitive processes (3.1.3)
- cognitive emulation can promote user acceptence (3.1.4)
- effective knowledge elicitation often requires psychologically-orientated techniques (3.1.5)

A more pragmatic attitude is called for: one that acknowledges both the potential usefulness and the limitations of cognitive emulation for knowledge engineering purposes. The next chapter considers factors likely to further constrain and facilitate a cognitive approach.

4

Factors facilitating and constraining cognitive emulation

The arguments reviewed in the previous chapter suggest that a significant degree of cognitive emulation is inherent in expert system design, but that a pure unselective strategy of emulation is both unrealistic and undesirable. In this chapter we discuss several rather more pragmatic considerations: some constraining, others facilitating, the viability of an emulation approach.

4.1 CONSTRAINTS ON COGNITIVE EMULATION

4.1.1 The emulability of human expertise in artificial systems

It is not yet clear what limits (if any) there are on modelling the cognitive processes underlying expert behaviour in an artificial system. This issue is essentially a specific instance of the wider debate about the comparative nature of artificial and human intelligence (e.g. Boden, 1977).

An influential development in this debate has been the notion of a "Physical Symbol System" proposed by Newell and Simon (1976). This notion defines a broad class of system capable of having and manipulating symbols, or more generally symbolic structures, yet that are realizable as physical entities. Newell and Simon's central hypothesis is that Physical Symbol Systems have all the necessary and sufficient means for intelligent action. In their view, human beings and computers are prime instances of such systems. If this meta-theory is correct then in principle there should be no limitation on cognitive emulation in expert systems.

On the other hand it may be, as some critics of AI contend, that in essential respects human cognitive processes cannot be adequately captured in computer programs (Searle, 1984; Weizenbaum, 1976). Clearly, if these critics prove right then the prospects for a modelling approach are poor.

It seems doubtful whether this fundamental issue can be resolved to universal satisfaction solely by resort to *a priori* arguments. Any "conclusive" argument is liable to be overthrown by empirical developments in cognitive psychology or the expert system field. An alternative view, intermediate between the two above, is that different aspects of human cognition vary in their emulability in computer systems. For example, cognitive scientists have found it relatively straightforward to simulate the acquisition of arithmetic skills using rule-based techniques (e.g. Young and O'Shea, 1981).

By contrast, reasoning by analogy and the representation of spatial concepts have proved difficult to model computationally (Hayes-Roth, 1984; Pinker, 1984). One underlying factor is the fundamental difficulty of simulating continuous mental processes by digital means, i.e. on digital computers (Sowa, 1984). Again, though, it is too early to tell whether aspects of expert thinking currently unamenable to emulation will remain so in the future. [This book adopts the working hypothesis that, in at least some significant respects, human cognition can be emulated on digital computers.]

4.1.2   The state of cognitive psychology

Another potential source of difficulty for system builders adopting a strategy of emulation stems from the current state of development of cognitive psychology. The difficulties for a modelling approach include:

(1) *Ignorance*

Despite a certain amount of progress, it is apparent that many key questions about human cognition have yet to be tackled, let alone answered, to general satisfaction. Norman (1981) maps out many of these gaps in our present knowledge of the human mind. Problem: One cannot emulate what is not known.

(2) *Diversity of approaches*

In Kuhnian terms psychology is an immature science, in a "pre-paradigmatic" stage of development (Boden, 1977). This is reflected in the confusingly varied range of theories, models, knowledge representation formalisms, etc. presented in the cognitive literature — often as explanations of the same phenomenon. Problem: Which theory/model/formalism does one choose to emulate?

(3) *Scientific Status*

As a science the theories and hypotheses of cognitive psychology are constantly subject to revision, obsolescence and falsification by empirical research findings (Popper, 1963). That is, our knowledge of human cognition is provisional in nature. Problem: The cognitive model emulated today may be refuted by later research.

(4) *Implementability*

The main criterion of an explanation's acceptability in cognitive psychology is experimental corroboration: in AI it is implementability (Hayes, 1984). As a consequence AI researchers have often found psychological models not sufficiently robust or predictive to implement as working programs. This problem has constrained expert systems research (Coombs and Alty, 1984; Hasling, Clancey and Rennels, 1984).

4.1.3 Expert systems technology

The existing technology for building expert systems — both hardware (e.g. Von Neumann architectures) and software (languages, shells and other system building tools) — is unequal to the task of modelling some influential and potentially useful ideas in cognitive psychology. [The tutorial article by Hayes-Roth (1984) provides a clear summary of the state of the art in knowledge engineering, and what notions it can handle.]

To take one example: "spreading activation" (e.g. Anderson, 1983a; Collins and Loftus, 1975). In this theory, memory is represented as a network of nodes. When one or more nodes become active (perhaps due to a sensory input or memory probe) activation spreads out in parallel to the nearest nodes, forming an expanding sphere of activation around the original node(s). Roughly speaking, activation decreases the further one gets from the initial source(s) of activation. Anderson (1983a) argues that activation can function as a 'relevancy heuristic', on the reasonable assumption that knowledge associated with what is being processed is likely to be relevant to that processing. However, spreading activation is essentially a parallel mechanism requiring parallel machinery for its efficient implementation. And "until such machinery becomes available, this potentially good idea will not see extensive use in pure artificial intelligence applications (applied knowledge engineering)" (Anderson, 1983a, p.88). This restriction applies equally to other cognitive mechanisms that are believed to be parallel processes (see Table 4.2).

On the software side, Hayes-Roth (1984) mentions analogues, meta-knowledge, naive physics and first principles as types of human knowledge not yet available in state-of-the-art expert systems. Table 4.2 provides other examples.

4.1.4 Individual variation in expert thinking

Cognitive psychologists seek to identify general principles of human thinking. Individual variation in cognitive performance is accounted for with reference to these principles. Whilst a strategy of cognitive emulation based purely on general principles of human (expert) cognition might be possible, such any approach has its limitations.

The cognitive research giving rise to generalizations about the human mind (and even the decision processes of a particular group of domain specialists), is usually based on experimental results gathered from many subjects and analyzed using standard statistical techniques. In cognitive simulation psychologists may thus model a "prototypical" or representative subject (Simon, 1979). From the point of view of cognitive emulation, the danger is that this kind of application of general principles will fail to do proper justice to the known richness and variety of reasoning strategies, knowledge representations, etc. of individual experts (Kuipers and Kassirer, 1984; Newell and Simon, 1972). The problem-solving capability of an expert program might suffer accordingly.

An alternative methodology for cognitive emulation is to model a system on the thinking of particular expert(s) using detailed techniques (e.g. protocol analysis). However, this is essentially what many knowledge engineers would claim to be doing already.

Perhaps the answer lies in combining these polar approaches. That is to say, eliciting knowledge from individual experts using standard knowledge acquisition techniques like interviewing and protocol analysis, followed by the tailoring of knowledge formalisms and inferencing methods (selected from a "toolkit" of psychologically plausible alternatives) to reflect the distinctive cognitive processes of individual experts. Unfortunately, the current state of expert systems technology (see Section 4.1.3) would not support such an application of the emulation principle at present.

4.1.5 Knowledge engineering objectives

The final constraining influence considered is that posed by the apparent conflict between a strategy of cognitive emulation and other knowledge engineering criteria. Textbooks (Barr and and Feigenbaum, 1981, 1982; Hayes-Roth, Waterman and Lenat, 1983) and review articles (e.g. Buchanan, 1982; Davis, 1982; Duda and Shortliffe, 1983) discuss various system design criteria. For present purposes only five are distinguished:

(1) *Efficiency*
To minimize costs and response times, knowledge engineers aim to build computer systems that are maximally efficient in their use of computational resources, i.e. memory, time.

(2) *Modifiability*
It is considered highly desirable that the knowledge embodied in an expert system be easy to add, delete and amend. This reflects the slow, iterative nature of the knowledge acquisition process, which typically requires numerous alterations and extensions to the knowledge stored in the system.

(3) *Simplicity*
Simplicity of design has several advantages. By keeping the knowledge representation, inferencing techniques, etc. as simple as possible, it is hoped that the resulting system will be easier to develop and maintain, cost less and be more intelligible.

(4) *Understandability*
Understandability is sought because it facilitates all stages of expert system construction, and, by making the basis of the system's behaviour more intelligible, helps promote user acceptance.

(5) *Correctness*
In order to achieve expert-level performance techniques yielding provably correct conclusions are favoured. Consistancy and completeness in the knowledge base is also sought. Moreover, users may express more confidence in the decisions of a system whose judgements are perceived as rationally derived.

Table 4.1 attempts to show how these five design criteria, together with the constraints on emulation discussed earlier, favour a variety of design features commonly found in expert systems. In Table 4.2 the same design features are related to psychological research on corresponding aspects of human (expert) cognition. From inspection of Table 4.2 it is apparent that many typical expert system features are highly implausible as models of how human experts think.

4.2   FACTORS FACILITATING COGNITIVE EMULATION

4.2.1   Developments in expert systems technology
In an earlier section (4.3.3) the current state of expert system technology was identified as an important constraint on cognitive

Table 4.1 — Knowledge engineering factors favouring typical expert system features

Expert system feature	Knowledge Engineering factor(s)	Comment
(1) Uniform Representation of Knowledge	Simplicity	Each formalism requires its own inferencing mechanism
	Efficiency	Computational resources needed to store and communicate between many formalisms
	Technology	Availability of uniform inplementation languages e.g. PROLOG
(2) Modular Representation of Knowledge	Modifiability	Enables knowledge to be added, deleted and amended with minimal effects on remainder of knowledge in system
(3) Natural Representation of Knowledge	Understandability	A declarative formalism such as rules can make the individual items of knowledge easier to understand
(4) Unrestricted Working Memory Capacity	Correctness	Potentially valuable facts, etc. could be lost maintaining limit on store size
	Understandability	Imposing a WM restriction might appear perverse or irrational to users
(5) Boolean Representation of Patterns	Simplicity	Imposes constrained format
	Efficiency	Boolean algebra very efficiently processed by digital computers
	Correctness	Guaranteed "correct" reasoning using Boolean algebra
	Technology	Psychological nature of pattern representation poorly understood
(6) Complete Pattern Matching	Simplicity	A more complex interpreter required to handle partial matching
	Correctness	Full matching requirement facilitates accuracy
(7) Probabilistic handling of Uncertainty	Correctness	Probabilistic methods offer the *promise* of accuracy (but see e.g. White, 1984).
	Technology	A range of established formal methods are available (e.g. Bayes Thereom, fuzzy set theory)
(8) Undirectional Control Structure	Simplicity	e.g. backward chaining nature of PROLOG
	Technology	The flexible intermixture of forward and backward reasoning characteristic of human thinking difficult to emulate
(9) Serial Processing	Technology	Parallel architectures still at the prototype stage
(10) Direct Manipulation of Knowledge	Modifiability	Ability to directly add, delete and alter units of knowledge required for ease of system development/maintenance
(11) Static Knowledge Base	Technology	Absence of techniques for dynamic changes to knowledge base whilst in use
(12) Reasoning-Based Explanation	Correctness	Accurate picture of how conclusions were reached
	Technology	Easy to implement e.g. rule-tracing

Table 4.2 — Typical expert system features and cognitive research findings

Expert system feature	Cognitive research findings	Selected references
(1) Uniform Represenation of Knowledge	Expert knowledge of many distinct types — indicating multiple representations. Basic distinction between declarative and procedural representation often made. Evidence for specialized representations of visual and spatial knowledge.	[Anderson (1983a), Gammack and Young (1984), Pinker (1984), Rumelhart and Norman (1983)]
(2) Modular Representation of Knowledge	Expertise in a domain characterized by integration of knowledge into larger units, be they chunks, scripts, themes [1], rules, etc. and by high interconnectivity between facts.	[Anderson (1983b), Chase and Simon (1973), Reder and Anderson (1980), Smith et al. (1978)]
(3) Natural Representation of Knowledge	Human expertise seems to rely heavily of procedurally embedded or "compiled" knowledge. Knowledge underlying cognitive performance (including experts') often not verbalizable.	[Anderson (1983b) Berry and Broadbent (1984), Rumelhart and Norman (1981)]
(4) Unrestricted Working Memory Cpacity	Experts have larger WMs for domain knowledge than novices. Nevertheless, experts' WMs still severely limited in number and complexity of items that can be held — imposing constraints on human information processing capacity.	[Chase and Ericsson (1982), Miller (1956), Newell and Simon (1972)]
(5) Boolean Representation of Patterns	Generally, patterns and concepts do not appear to be represented in cognition as simple predicates linked in arbitrary arrangements by the Boolean operators "or", "and" and "not" e.g. negation rarely used, "integral" [2] and structural patterns difficult to represent.	[Barsalou and Bower (1984), Garner (1976), Hayes-Roth (1978), Johnson-Laird and Wason (1977)]
(6) Complete Pattern Matching	Humans adept at coping with missing or incorrect information in pattern matching e.g. classifying novel instances on the basis of their similarity to other category instances or category prototype [3].	[Barsalou and Bower (1984), Elio and Anderson (1981), Posner and Keele (1970)]
(7) Probabilistic Handling of Uncertainty	People, including experts, appear to rely heavily on nonstatistical heuristics e.g. availability and representativeness in making judgements under uncertainty. Human experts influenced by more qualitative (e.g. configurational) aspects of data.	[Anderson (1983a), Chi, et al. (1981), Larkin et al. (1980), Shriffin and Schneider (1977)]
(8) Undirectional Control Structure	Compared with novices, the performance of human experts is often more dependent on data-driven processes e.g. pattern recognition. But generally expert thinking seems characterized by a flexible intermixture of forward and backward reasoning.	[Anderson (1983a), Chi, et al. (1981), Larkin et al. (1980) Shiffrin and Schneider (1977)]
(9) Serial Processing	Automated cognitive processes such as pattern recognition, memory retrieval and other more specialized skills, e.g. reading, appear essentially parallel in nature.	[McClennand and Rumelhart, (1981), Neisser (1976), Shiffrin and Schneider (1977)]
(10) Direct Manipulation of Knowledge	Research suggests procedural knowledge first represented declaratively as facts, and only becomes proceduralized through repeated use or practice. Once "compiled", knowledge not readily deleted or modified.	[Anderson, (1983a,b), Larkin (1981)]
(11) Static Knowledge Base	Human knowledge is dynamic in that it has the ability to recode, restructure and generally modify itself in "real-time".	[Bartlett (1932), Chi et al. (1981), Rumelhart and Norman (1978)]
(12) Reasoning-Based Explanation	Cognitive processes underlying expert performance often difficult to explain. Instead, experts may base their explanations on causal reasoning using domain models and principles, or even post-hoc rationalizations.	[Berry and Broadbent (1984), Nisbett and Wilson (1977), Wason and Evans (1975)]

Terms:

[1] *Themes* A term used to denote a thematically integrated set of facts in declarative memory (Anderson, 1983a; Reder and Anderson, 1980).

[2] *Integral pattern* A class of stimuli that are not analysed into independent attributes (e.g. colour, size) in cognition, but are processed in a holistic manner (Garner, 1976).

[3] *Category prototype* The best or clearest example of a category. For example, a robin probably conforms to most people's idea of a typical "bird", whereas a vulture does not (Posner and Keele, 1970; Rosch, 1977).

Other terms are explained elsewhere in this book (see index).

emulation. However, the technology is still in an early phase of development (Bramer, 1984). Over the next decade or two, the massive world-wide investment in fifth-generation research projects should remove at least some of the technological constraints on modelling human cognition. The development of parallel architectures is an obvious example on the hardware side (Bishop, 1986). Regarding software, research and development objectives include multi-representation systems, model-based reasoning, meta-knowledge systems and learning by example (Hayes-Roth, 1984).

4.2.2 Cognitive research

In addition to providing constraints on a strategy of cognitive emulation (see Section 4.3.2), cognitive psychology can facilitate the strategy in several ways:

- *Cognitive psychology has "heuristic value"*. That is, the psychological literature on human thinking can serve as a useful source of ideas for expert system builders. So, for example, there is a degree of consensus amongst cognitive psychologists regarding certain broad principles of human information processing (some of these are referred to in Table 4.2). And concerning the cognitive processes subsuming human expertise, a growing body of research findings is available (see Chapter 2).
- *The advent of cognitive science*. Some researchers in cognitive psychology and related disciplines (AI, philosophy, linguistics, etc.) now identify themselves as Cognitive Scientists. Amongst other things, this label denotes a commitment to implementing and testing cognitive ideas as computational models (Slack, 1984). This requirement ought to make the task of cognitive emulation in expert programs that much easier.
- *Developments in the subject*. The ongoing research effort by cognitive psychologists should significantly advance our understanding of the human mind in general, and expert cognition in particular. And such advances, if computationally expressed, would provide a more assured basis for adopting the cognitive emulation principle.

4.2.3 Cognitive emulation can coincide with other knowledge engineering objectives

In Tables 4.1 and 4.2 the emphasis is on areas of conflict. Nevertheless, it is apparent that cognitive emulation will sometimes coincide rather than conflict with other systems design criteria:

- Knowledge-based and rule-based techniques. These were discussed earlier (Section 3.1.1).

● Cognitive emulation would overlap with other criteria (e.g. development cost and effort) if it helped overcome the bottleneck in knowledge acquisition (see Section 3.1.5).

● Cognitive emulation can coincide with computational efficiency. In one reported study of machine induction, a hierarchially structured set of rules (so structured for greater understandability) were induced more efficiently than a single very large decision rule based on the original ID3 algorithm (see Michie, 1982). Moreover, encoding expert knowledge naturally as pattern-based rules can help control the explosion of combinatorial complexity that more formal approaches might entail (Michie, 1980).

● Knowing the appropriate rule size for human reasoning can also help in knowledge elicitation from the expert (Welbank, 1983).

● To provide an expert system with a sophisticated natural language interface may require the interface having access to the expert system's knowledge and operations, implying that these must be represented in an appropriate (humanlike?) form (Sparck Jones, 1984).

● Well-known cognitive principles are already being applied to "humanising" the man–machine interface of expert systems (see Welbank, 1983). An awareness of the limitations on people's capacity to process information underlies Donald Michie's (Michie, 1980) recommendation that expert systems be designed to include a "human window", i.e. employ a conceptualization of knowledge and inferencing techniques that can be both understood and executed by a human user. Such a facility is considered vital for systems employed in high-risk applciation areas like nuclear plant management.

4.2.4   Problems unamenable to formal methods

The intractible nature of a problem using formal (ie. non-cognitive) techniques, could facilitate more psychologically-oriented approaches — even though this might clash with other design criteria. To date, the relatively limited range, complexity and size of tasks tackled by expert systems has usually enabled expert-level performance to be achieved without significantly compromising system design criteria such as correctness, efficiency, etc. So, for example, the existing technology has proved sufficient for handling such "analytic" tasks as medical diagnosis and geological classification (especially in small, well-defined domains). [Stefik *et al.* (1982) have suggested a set of architectural prescriptions for building expert systems of this type, which makes use of current techniques.]

However, many leading practitioneers in the expert system field (e.g. Davis, 1982; Duda and Shortliffe, 1983; Hayes-Roth, 1984), suggest that current techniques may prove inadequate for handling the much larger knowledge bases (containing several million facts), more varied tasks (e.g. "synthetic" tasks like design) and more complex capabilities (e.g. learning from experience) predicted for future applications. Since the human mind has proved equal to coping with such tasks, whereas formal AI techniques have not as yet, an opportunity for a cognitive approach exists here.

Broadly speaking, the utility of the cognitive emulation principle might be expected to increase as the tasks tackled by expert system builders become more difficult.

4.3   SUMMARY AND CONCLUSIONS

Several constraints on cognitive emulation were identified: Some cognitive processes may not be amenable to emulation in principle. Others may be emulable in principle, but not with the available technology. Our current understanding of human cognition is incomplete, with many competing explanations and the prospect of established notions being falsified. The individual variation in expert cognition may not map comfortably onto general principles derived from cognitive research. Special attention was given on the way in which cognitive emulation could conflict with established knowledge engineering objectives such as efficiency and modifiability.

Factors considered likely to facilitate a cognitive approach include: future developments in expert systems technology and the cognitive sciences, situations where cognitive emulation coincides with other design criteria, and the need to tackle problems intractable using formal methods.

Whether it is feasible to explicitly adopt a strategy of cognitive emulation will depend on the particular balance of facilitating and constraining factors operating in any given instance. Fig. 4.1 provides a rough-and-ready decision rule based on the points raised in this chapter. Applying this rule, the state of the "enabling" technologies and disciplines would seem to weigh against all but a highly selective pursuit of cognitive emulation for commercial applications at the present time. In the longer term, however, the decision rule implies that a combination of developments in expert systems techno-

If

| 1. | Existing (formal) techniques cannot meet all major knowledge engineering requirements for an application satisfactorily |

and

| 2. | Cognitive process(es) can be identified that appear relevant to meeting the application requirements |

and

| 3. | Cognitive process(es) involved considered emulable in principle |

and

| 4. | Cognitive process(es) involved psychologically understood |

and

| 5. | Cognitive process(es) involved available as a computational model |

and

| 6.1 | Knowledge engineering tools embodying cognitive process(es) commercially available |

and

| 6.2 | Resources available to develop knowledge engineering tools embodying cognitive process(es) |

and

| 7. | Knowledge engineering tools embodying (generalized) cognitive process(es) can be tailored to expressively accommodate knowledge, etc. elicited from individual domain experts |

and

| 8.1 | Emulating cognitive process(es) *does* significantly compromise other knowledge engineering objectives (e.g. efficiency) |

or

| 8.2.1 | Emulating cognitive process(es) *does not* significantly compromise other knowledge engineering objectives (e.g. efficiency) |

and

| 8.2.2 | Problem unsolvable using alternative techniques |

then

Cognitive process(es) involved should be emulated in an expert system.

Fig. 4.1 — A decision rule for adopting a strategy of cognitive emualtion in expert system design.

logy and cognitive science, the need to tackle larger and more difficult problems, the desire to further humanize the user interface, etc. will make adopting a strategy of cognitive emulation increasingly attractive — if not essential.

5

Applications of the emulation principle: A survey of approaches

5.1 GENERAL INTRODUCTION

The two previous chapters have considered the formal arguments for and against cognitive emulation, and some of the practical issues involved. We reached the interim conclusion that cognitive emulation is an inherent feature of design, but that an unselective strategy of emulation is both unrealistic and undesirable. Some of the circumstances in which a strategy of emulation might be useful were also noted. In this chapter we aim to draw out in more detail the implications of the strategy for such issues as knowledge acquisition, knowledge representation and system architecture. And through an examination of different applications of the emulation principle, it will hopefully become clearer that a workable and coherent approach to expert system design is being discussed.

These aims are achieved through a survey of work in expert systems, and closely related fields, which have addressed the emulation issue. What such a survey reveals is that cognitive emulation is far from constituting a unitary design strategy. On the contrary, as instanced by the published literature, it is more aptly viewed as a loosely bundled set of approaches that share a (variable) commitment to emulating human cognition. This point can be illustrated by a series of quotes from the knowledge engineering literature. The following statements form an approximate continuum — the first quotes express no concern for cognitive emulation; those towards the end advocate a strong version of the strategy:

[1] ... expert system: a computer program which uses artificial

intelligence (AI) techniques to do the same task as a human expert does. (Welbank, 1983, p. 1)

[2] ... an expert system is a set of computer programs which emulates human expertise by applying techniques of logical inference to a knowledge base. (Johnson, 1984, p. 15)

[3] It is essential to model the expert's inference structure ... but not as important to model the search process he uses. (Clancey, 1984, p. 13)

[4] The knowledge representation and control strategy selected should accurately reflect what the human expert knows and how he uses that knowledge to solve a problem. This does not mean that the system has to be a psychological model ... but it does mean that the representation chosen must be able to capture the fullest range and power of the human expert's knowledge in that particular domain. (Kidd, 1985a, p. 243)

[5] Cognitive emulation is an expert system design strategy that attempts to model system performance on human (expert) thinking. (Slatter, 1985, p.28)

[6] Cognitive emulation means building systems in such a way that they process information in ways that resemble how users process information. (Fox, 1983, p. 8)

[7] Unless there is a clear reason not to an expert system should be designed to process information in ways that approximate human information processing as closely as possible. (Fox, 1982, p.4)

[1] and [2] are standard technical definitions. They imply only that human expert *performance* should be emulated — and then by using formal AI techniques. [3] and [4] manifest an intermediate commitment: [3] is selective in which aspect of human cognition it considers it is necessary to emulate, whereas [4] suggests that it is sufficient to capture the *functionality* of expert cognition. [5], [6] and [7] offer the strongest endorsements of the cognitive emulation principle.

The above quotes serve to illustrate another dimension along which approaches to emulation may be tentatively categorized, i.e. the level of generality at which the emulation issue is addressed. So, for example, some approaches emphasize the emulation of individual experts [3]. Others are more concerned with emulating the cognitive processes representative of larger aggregates of people — experts in a particular domain [4], "experts" [5], "users" [6], or human cognition in general [7]. The survey in this chapter is organized around this framework, which is illustrated in Fig. 5.1. The number in brackets next to each approach refers to the section in which that approach is discussed.

Some preliminary remarks about this scheme are in order. First of

Level	Broad approach to cognitive emulation	
Human population large	Emulating "human information processing" (5.6)	Emulating "neural" processing (5.7)
Large group level	Emulating "user" cognition (5.5)	Emulating "expert" cognition (5.4)
Small group level		Emulating expertise of experts in a particular domain (5.3)
Single person level		Emulating the individual expert (5.2)

Fig. 5.1 — Approaches to cognitive emulation at different levels of generality.

all, it is not intended to be exhaustive. In particular, such important topics as vision and natural language understanding, for which human cognition provides one obvious model, and which may figure prominently in the expert systems of the future, are outside the scope of the present survey. Our coverage is limited to the core expert system topics of reasoning and control strategies, knowledge representation, knowledge acquisition and system architecture.

Second, the six approaches cited in Fig. 5.1 are clearly not mutually exclusive. Thus, for example, it is quite reasonable to attempt to emulate both user and expert cognition within a single system. Or again, an approach to cognitive emulation inspired by a cognitive model of how human expertise develops may still need instantiating with respect to a particular domain, and individual experts within that domain (cf. Kolodner, 1984). It is usually possible, however, to identify the approach(es) which provide(s) the main rationale for any given attempt at emulation.

Each of the six approaches is outlined and evaluated in turn. In most cases, each broad approach comprises several distinctive research and development efforts, which are described separately. As indicated in Fig. 5.1 we start by considering the least general approaches. This is because these connect most readily with the everyday concerns of knowledge engineers — how to capture, represent and use the knowledge of individual experts, or formalize the expertise within a particular domain.

A major concern of the chapter is to make explicit the contrasting implications for expert systems design of these different approaches to emulation. This is a vital issue since the satisfaction of different knowledge engineering objectives (efficiency, modifiability, intelligibility) may well require that two or more approaches to emulation are combined within a single system. Some of the conflicts that can arise are explored in the discussion section (5.8). We also sketch some tentative solutions.

5.2 EMULATING INDIVIDUAL EXPERTS

5.2.1 Introduction

Emulating human cognition at the level of an individual expert clearly has implications for the way knowledge is represented and deployed in an expert system, and for the overall architecture of the system. But questions about knowledge representation, knowledge utilization and architecture arise naturally at other levels of emulation also; so discussion of these issues will be deferred until later. Instead, we focus here on that aspect of cognitive emulation which can be addressed only at the level of individual experts — knowledge elicitation. [By knowledge elicitation is meant knowledge acquisition activities where the source of information is a human expert.] The section is organized around a discussion of what makes knowledge elicitation difficult. This is a key issue, since effective emulation is critically dependent on the quantity and quality of elicited knowledge. We start by outlining some of the practical difficulties that knowledge engineers can face. Verbal data collected in one way or another is an essential part of knowledge elicitation: the limitations of this source of data are outlined. Inaccessibility of certain types of knowledge is one potential limitation. We consider whether there are kinds of human knowledge that are unelicitable in principle. Whether there are or not, the problem is compounded by the use of techniques unsuited to eliciting particular types of expert knowledge. The final constraint on effective cognitive emulation during knowledge elicitation to be considered is that imposed by the use of inappropriate representational and inferencing tools.

5.2.2 Practical difficulties in knowledge elicitation

These are dealt with at length elsewhere (e.g. Welbank, 1983), and include:

● Knowledge elicitation techniques are poorly understood. Compared with the topic of knowledge representation, the discussion of knowledge acquisition in the expert systems literature has, at least until the last year or two, been rather sparse.

● Lack of relevant training and experience amongst knowledge engineers in the available knowledge elicitation techniques.
● The inaccessibility of experts. They are usually very busy people, in high demand within an organization.
● Experts may be unenthusiastic. For example, they may feel threatened by the purpose of the project, or take exception to the attitude of the knowledge engineer. This puts a premium on interpersonal skills, in order to motivate the expert and retain goodwill and co-operation.

Practical problems such as these can seriously distort attempts at emulation. Further research into knowledge elicitation and improved training of knowledge engineers would help enormously.

5.2.3   Limitations of verbal data

It is a misconception to suppose that knowledge can be directly captured (or "mined") from a domain expert. All that knowledge elicitation techniques such as interviews and protocols can capture is a series of verbal utterances. It is the knowledge engineer who, through the interpretive processes of sifting, selection, re-representation, etc., converts this verbal data into the modules of knowledge that most expert systems require. Breuker and Wielinga (1983a) have described several of the sources of invalidity in verbal data which are worth restating here:

● the expert's inexperience in self-report techniques
● reconstruction/theorizing   rather   than   accurate   reporting ("gap-filling")
● inaccessibility of procedural knowledge
● the ineffability of certain events or internal representations
● lack of ecological validity in the eliciting context (e.g. giving a verbal protocol on an unrepresentative task)
● the taken-for-grantedness of highly familiar knowledge
● straightforward forgetting of relevant information
● ambiguities in verbalizations
● secrecy and deliberate under-reporting.

A partial solution to the invalidity of verbal data is to be found in the iterative, feedback-driven nature of expert system construction, which facilitates the detection and correction of shortcomings in the system's knowledge base. And we shall be considering other remedial measures in the next three sections. However, it is hard to conceive of an approach to the elicitation and interpretation of verbal data that would guarantee the completeness and accuracy of the resulting knowledge base. To this extent a fundamental limitation on emulation of individual experts must be accepted.

5.2.4   Unelicitable knowledge?

In the previous section the inaccessibility of certain types of human knowledge was cited as one source of invalidity in verbal data. And earlier, in Chapter 2, we noted that human *expert* knowledge tends to be even less accessible, due to the proceduralisation of task-related knowledge that takes place as expertise develops. This raises the question of whether there may exist types of human knowledge that are unelicitable in principle.

The notion of tacit knowledge has figured prominently in discussions of this subject. One such claim has recently been made by Collins, Green and Draper (1985):

> The mistake is to think that if knowledge elicitation tools and techniques are sufficiently refined, and if enough time and diligence are dedicated to the task, the whole of an expert's knowledge can be elicited. This is untrue; one cannot elicit that which no-one knows that they know — that which they cannot articulate. (p. 328)

The notion of tacit knowledge was first developed in philosophy by Polyani (see Boden, 1977, for a summary). It refers to the tacit inferences and global knowledge that provide a nonarticulable framework for human reasoning, including expert reasoning. Collins *et al.* (1985) make the worthwhile point that a skilled user might be able to compensate for the absence of tacit knowledge in a knowledge base by supplying his own when interpreting an expert system's behaviour. Regarding the wider issue of whether tacit knowledge is elicitable in principle, Polyani himself suggested that it was in fact formalizable (Boden, 1977, p. 435).

Further clarification can be achieved by distinguishing between, on the one hand, nonarticulatable (or nonverbalizable) knowledge and, on the other, unelicitable knowledge. That is, it may be possible to elicit (or infer) knowledge that an expert cannot give direct verbal expression to by using, say, techniques derived from cognitive psychology. Machine induction of decision rules from examples supplied and classified by the expert can play a similar role.

In conclusion, the contention that some aspects of human knowledge are not elicitable in principle has yet to be demonstrated. But even if *all* human knowledge were elicitable in principle, the severe practical problems of eliciting inaccessible knowledge would remain.

5.2.5   The use of inappropriate elicitation techniques

Another diagnosis of why knowledge acquisition represents a major bottleneck in expert system development stresses the use of inappropriate elicitation techniques. For example, informal interviews may be the only technique employed, despite their unsuitability for eliciting certain types of knowledge (Gammack and Young, 1984). Table 5.1 summarizes six major knowledge acquisition techniques that are currently available; Table 5.2 suggests how these techniques may most suitably be deployed in capturing different types of knowledge.

Once it is accepted that even within a single specialist domain expertise can comprise several distinctive types of knowledge, the need for a variety of elicitation techniques becomes evident (Gammack and Young, 1984; Kidd, 1985b). The problem is then one of how best to match techniques to knowledge types. Table 5.2 is just one attempt to do this.

In summary, for eliciting the deeper, more "psychological" types of knowledge upon which effective cognitive emulation depends, a range of techniques needs to be deployed. No one technique is sufficient for all purposes.

5.2.6   The use of inappropriate expert system development tools

Knowledge engineers have to work with the expert system development tools at their disposal. However, the limitations of existing software can seriously distort the knowledge elicitation process. For example, the use of, say, an EMYCIN-type shell presents the knowledge engineer with a predetermined format into which elicited data must be made to fit. Because a variant on the rule formalism is the only knowledge representation supported in some commercial expert system software, there is a real danger that types of knowledge not conveniently expressible in the available formalism will have to be either represented in an unnatural way or discarded altogether (cf. Gammack and Young, 1984). Knowledge engineers may also be encouraged in the misconception that only rules and facts are important in expert system building, and that other types of knowledge can safely be ignored (Kidd, 1985b).

The requirements of the inference engine can exert their own influence on knowledge elicitation. Thus the use of a backward chaining shell may encourage the knowledge engineer to ask "where are the goals?"

How can the distorting effect of available software be countered? Clearly, in the long term expert software which can naturally accommodate the full range of human knowledge types and inferenc-

Table 5.1 — Overview of six knowledge elicitation techniques

(1) INTERVIEWS	The most familiar method. Widely used because it is relaxed and acceptable. Can take many forms: e.g. asking expert to give introductory lecture or tutorial about the task domain, or the interview can incorporate techniques used in cognitive psychology for probing memory such as "critical incident reports". The interview may follow a fixed plan of questioning predetermined by the knowledge engineer, or be unstructured, with the expert allowed to ramble.
advantages	Reckoned to be useful early on for eliciting the basic structure of a domain. A lot of knowledge which is explicit to the expert can be elicited quickly. Relatively easy.
disadvantages	Unsuited for eliciting detailed or inaccessible domain knowledge. Time consuming: e.g. preparing interview plan, transcribing recordings of interview. Relies heavily on uncued recall, which is poor.
(2) VERBAL PROTOCOLS	The expert is required to give a verbal commentary on what he or she is thinking about whilst working through a problem. A recording is made of this "verbal protocol" which is transcribed and analysed. In the classic psychological method at least, this can result in a set of production rules which, when executed, simulate the person's problem solving strategy. A less time-consuming variant on the classical method employed by Myers *et al.* (1983) involved highlighting the substantive knowledge in the transcript using a text editor, and coding it directly into rules to form a prototype expert system.
advantages	More natural task situation. Permits inference of knowledge the expert cannot directly verbalize, especially the expert's procedures. Useful where preselected examples exist.
disadvantages	Giving protocol can interfere with task performance. Protocol analysis a skilled and difficult task; laborious. Transcript can be highly ambiguous, requiring much "interpretation" when analysed.
(3) MACHINE INDUCTION	Machine-induced rules often have little resemblance to those elicited from human experts using other techniques. However, it is appropriate to consider machine induction as a technique for facilitating cognitive emulation for two reasons. First, the large example sets fed in as raw data are selected and preclassified by human experts, reflecting their conceptualization of a domain. Second, there is some evidence (e.g. Bratko *et al.* 1985) that induced rules can approximate human rules under favourable conditions such as having a complete or highly representative set of examples.
advantages	Only needs preclassified examples. Can cut out the need for a knowledge engineer. Will account for all examples.
disadvantages	Require a database of documented cases, structured around human knowledge.

ing strategies must be the objective. As a practical short-term measure, the coding of knowledge into an intermediate represen-

	Instability — a single example can radically change an induced rule.
	Induced rules are often large and complex, leading to intelligibility problems.
(4) OBSERVA-TIONAL STUDIES	Similar to verbal protocols, except that there is no interference to the expert's normal task performance from a secondary activity (giving a verbal report). It can take such forms as videoing, the recording of phone conversations between engineers and remote users, or recordings of radio "help" programmes (e.g. Kidd, 1985c). Whatever the medium, the transcripts require detailed analysis for useful knowledge to be extracted.
advantages	Helps overcome preconceived ideas.
	Can find out what the expert's role is and what the expert actually does.
	If a user involved, draws attention to their contribution (often overlooked).
disadvantages	Makes heavy demand on knowledge engineer's time and resources.
	Can be a highly sensitive activity, making co-operation harder to get.
	Need to have a clear idea in advance of what to do with transcripts.
(5) CONCEPTUAL SORTING	A technique employed in cognitive psychology. At its simplest the task can involve: (a) obtaining a set of concepts that roughly covers a domain (from, say, a textbook or glossary); (b) transferring each concept to a card; (c) asking expert to sort cards into several groups, identifying what each group has in common; and (d) iteratively combining these groups to form a hierarchy.
advantages	Useful where there is a lot of information to be organized.
	Considered suitable for establishing global structure of domain knowledge.
	Statistical procedures such as cluster analysis may be applicable.
disadvantages	Requires some specialist skill to administer.
	Risk of producing artificially hierarchical structure of domain concepts.
(6) MULTI-DIMENSIONAL SCALING (MDS)	In psychology, MDS techniques are used to identify perceived similarities and differences in a set of concepts. The Repertory Grid Technique (RGT) is one such technique that has transferred successfully to knowledge engineering (e.g. Boose, 1984; Shaw and Gaines, 1983;). In contrast to conceptual sorting, which helps identify the broad conceptual structure, MDS techniques can uncover those fine discriminations between closely related concepts that experts make and which novices find hard to differentiate.
advantages	Good for eliciting subtle (nonverbal) distinctions between concepts.
	RGT of proven value as a knowledge elicitation technique.
disadvantages	Demanding on the expert if the number of inter-concept comparisons gets large.
	Statistical expertise required to understand and employ MDS techniques correctly.

Main Sources: Gammack and Young (1984), Kidd (1985b), Welbank (1983).

tation independent of any implementation appears useful. The detailed analysis of elicited knowledge at various levels of abstraction

Table 5.2 — Possible elicitation techniques for different types of knowledge

Type of knowledge	Interviews	Verbal protocols	Machine induction	Observ. studies	Conceptual sorting	MDS
Facts	×					
Heuristics		×	×			
Concepts/ relations	×					×
Classificatory knowledge			×		×	×
Meta- knowledge					×	
Problem negotiation				×		
User characteristics	×			×		
Procedural knowledge		×		×		
Tacit knowledge		×	×			×

Main sources: Breuker and Wielinga (1984), Gammack and Young (1984), Kidd (1985b).

is another relevant technique, which is discussed in more detail in Section 5.3.

5.2.7 Concluding remarks

To emulate the thinking of a human expert, his or her expertise must first be captured. We have reviewed several problems in knowledge elicitation that make effective emulation difficult. These ranged from the more tractable problems associated with lack of training amongst knowledge engineers and the use of unsuitable elicitation techniques and software tools, to the fundamental constraints imposed by the inherent limitations of verbal data and the inaccessible nature of certain types of human knowledge. Our purpose has been to suggest that through the use of appropriate remedial measures it is possible to capture much of the detail of expert thinking.

5.3 EMULATING DOMAIN EXPERTISE

5.3.1 Introduction

The organizing principle of this chapter is the emulation of human cognition at different levels of generality. In the previous section we considered emulation at the level of the individual domain specialist (focusing on the question of how effectively an expert's knowledge can be elicited). This section moves up a level of generality (see Fig. 5.1) to review approaches concerned with emulating *domain* expertise; i.e. approaches that seek to capture what is typical about the organization of knowledge and problem solving within a particular specialist area. The psychological validity of such endeavours derives from the domain-specific nature of expert cognition, which was discussed in Chapter 2.

Medical expertise in general, and clinical diagnostic skill in particular, has received the most attention in the published literature. Researchers have sought to embody clinical expertise in computer systems for two main reasons. First, to gain a better understanding of clinical cognition, with the aim of improving it. Second, to develop practical decision support tools for everyday medical use. The application of AI techniques in medicine has yielded a number of experimental programs that seriously attempt to emulate aspects of clinical cognition: INTERNIST (Pople 1982), NEOMYCIN (Clancey and Letsinger, 1981), PIP (Pauker *et al.* 1976) and PSYCO (Fox, Barber and Bardhan, 1980) are four prominent examples.

Three distinctive approaches to the simulation of (clinical) domain expertise are considered in this section:

(1) Simulation programs that mimic the behaviour of human clinicians.
(2) An alternative approach based on inferring an expert's reasoning by watching.
(3) Knowledge-oriented approaches, concerned with analysing the typical organization of knowledge within a domain.

5.3.2 Behavioural mimicry

Two major programs that fall under this category are INTERNIST and PIP. INTERNIST (Pople, 1982) is a large advisory program capable of making diagnoses in most areas of general internal medicine. It was modelled on one particular clinical expert (Myers). PIP, or Present Illness Program (Pauker *et al.*, 1976), models the way a human clinician takes down the Present Illness of a patient with edema — a procedure that includes diagnosis.

Insights derived from introspection and the observation of experienced clinicians provide the initial basis for such programs. Discrepancies between the behaviour of the system and the performance of the expert prompts an iterative cycle of testing and revising of the program. The cycle terminates when the behaviour of the program closely *mimics* that of a human expert over a range of test cases.

In short, such programs employ AI techniques of knowledge

representation, inferencing, etc. to simulate clinical cognition through behavioural mimicry. These programs do not explicitly attempt to implement models of expert thinking taken from the cognitive literature. Nevertheless, the approach can result in programs that incorporate many psychologically plausible features. This is true of PIP (Pauker *et al.* 1976) for example; whose features include:

- A system architecture comprising a short-term memory (STM), long-term memory (LTM) and control program (see Section 5.6 below).
- LTM organized as an *associative network* and packaged into frames.
- Hypothesize-and-test diagnostic strategy (see Chapter 2).
- Testing hypotheses by their "degree of fit" (e.g. *partial matching*) to disease *prototypes* (see Table 4.2).
- *Advoidance of backtracking*. The high interconnectedness of entities in LTM supports a lateral switching between hypotheses.
- Frames in LTM are either dormant, semi-activated or fully-activated. *Activation* is triggered by data in STM. This can be seen as a crude analogue to the psychological theory of "spreading activation" (See Section 4.1.3).

Against these plausible features, PIP also contains instances of many of the psychologically implausible features of expert systems cited in Table 4.2, including:

- A complex scoring system for computing numerical likelihoods used in hypothesis testing.
- Unnatural shifts in "attention" during information acquisition from the user (due to the peculiarities of the focusing scoring mechanism).
- No theoretical limit on STM storage capacity.
- Serial processing only.

Stepping back from the evaluation of one particular program, several difficulties with the behavioural mimicry approach in general are apparent. First, accurate mimicry of expert behaviour provides no gaurantee that the system is reasoning in the same way as the human expert (Wilkins, Buchanan and Clancey, 1984). Second, the published accounts of these systems often show a lack of awareness of the psychological literature on human decision making, with the step from observation of behaviour to design decisions poorly documented.

Before leaving the topic of behavioural mimicry, a variant on the approach ought to be noted. This can be illustrated by a medical diagnostic system reported by Reggia, Nau and Wang (1984). The performance of the program appears to correspond quite well with descriptions of clinical behaviour in the empirical literature. In the present context, the important point about this program is that it has a firm mathematical basis, being based on work in set theory. Reggia *et al.*'s program demonstrates that mathematical models can be successfully applied to explaining expert performance in a particular domain. There must, however, be a question mark over the psychological validity of mathematically inspired approaches, since they are essentially at odds with the types of explanation of expert cognition currently favoured by cognitive psychologists (see Chapter 2).

5.3.3 Inferring an expert's reasoning by watching
Wilkins *et al.* (1984) have proposed an alternative approach to emulating clinical expertise that addresses some of the weaknesses of behavioural mimicry. Wilkins *et al.* introduce a system designed to infer automatically the mental model of an expert medical diagnostician by watching how the expert diagnoses a patient. This work is primarily an attempt to solve the knowledge acquisition bottleneck by modelling the knowledge organization and acquisition methods of a program on human expertise. Medicine is a suitable domain for such an experiment because of the large research literature on clinical expertise.

Wilkins *et al.* point out that experts in many domains share an ability to infer the reasons for a colleague's decisions by watching their task performance. In particular, the ability to learn by watching appears important to the acquisition of medical expertise. In the early phases of medical training, the student studies and acquires textbook knowledge about human physiology and diseases. But at this stage real diagnostic competence has yet to be attained. There follows a period of apprenticeship during which the student observes experienced clinicians handling real diagnostic cases, and tries to duplicate this diagnostic skill when dealing with cases on their own. According to Wilkins *et al.* the ability to infer reasoning by watching is as basic a dimension of human expert skill as problem solving, explanations of expertise, or teaching of expertise.

The presented system is designed to acquire new domain knowledge in the following way:

(1) The system is supplied with a model of clinical reasoning (to provide the constraints necessary to infer the expert's model).
(2) The system watches a physician–patient consultation and

attempts to infer the expert's reason for asking a question at each point during the session.

(3) Whenever it cannot do so, the system concludes that the expert possesses some knowledge that it does not, and sets about trying to acquire the knowledge.

(4) Where the program fails to correctly infer the expert's model, protocol analysis is used to identify where the program is deficient.

(5) Changes are made to the program's domain-independent strategic knowledge (held separately from the domain knowledge).

Others are experimenting with this approach. For example, Boyle (1985) presents a modification of Wilkins *et al.*'s system to acquire both control and domain knowledge in a blackboard environment.

Assessment of the learning by watching approach is hampered because of the early stage of research efforts. But, in general, it compares favourably with behavioural mimicry. At least in the case of Wilkins *et al.*'s system, an attempt is made to base the system's knowledge organization and inferencing method on a model of clinical reasoning. And changes in the program are made in a more principled fashion. Wilkins *et al.* point out some of the weaknesses of the watching approach themselves: Individual differences between the reasoning styles of physicians can cause problems. Program failures may sometimes occur that are beyond the current state of cognitive psychology and expert systems technology to resolve; for example, situations involving complex temporal reasoning. A criticism about how these programs acquire knowledge is also in order, since their reliance on a single human-like strategy — inferring by watching — ignores the other means by which human expertise is acquired (see Chapter 2).

5.3.4 Knowledge-oriented approaches

We now turn to a third approach to emulating domain expertise, which focuses on achieving high-level representations of expert knowledge within a particular domain. In constructing expert systems it is useful to examine the knowledge to be embodied in the system at several levels. One notable classification (see Wielinga and Breuker, 1984, pp. 10–11) suggests knowledge can be analysed at at least five levels:

● Linguistic — the level at which the expert reports on his or her knowledge.

● Conceptual — the formalization of domain knowledge that unifies the knowledge of several experts, and perhaps several sub-domains, within a single conceptual framework.

● Epistemological — this level of analysis is designed to uncover the underlying structural properties of domain knowledge. It is expressed in epistemological primitives representing the basic elements, relations, strategies, etc.

● Logical — refers to the formalism(s) in which the knowledge is presented and upon which inferencing procedures operate.

● Implementational — an analysis in terms of the implementation language to be adopted.

Wielinga and Breuker (1984) point out that much research in expert systems has been concerned with mapping knowledge at the first (linguistic) level directly into an implementation language. The failure to analyse knowledge at any of the intervening levels — in particular, the epistemological level — may be at the root of several knowledge engineering problems:

(a) *Knowledge acquisition.* From linguistic data to implementation language is too large a gap to have to bridge in a single step; and valuable additional knowledge may be lost by not analysing at intermediate levels (Wielinga and Breuker, 1984).

(b) *Expert system design and modification.* The mixture of terms that is generally used to describe expert systems can confuse implementation language with knowledge structure and the search process. Clancey (1984) argues that this confusion makes it difficult to analyse new problems or derive a set of knowledge engineering principles. Furthermore, knowledge which has not been analysed at an epistemological level can prove difficult to modify by other than the original authors — a point brought out by Clancey (1983) in his examination of MYCIN's rule base.

(c) *Teaching and explanation.* Clancey (1983) also showed that his initial difficulties in adapting the MYCIN rule base to support a teaching and explanatory role were due to the proceduralized form of MYCIN rules. Clancey found that by uncovering the strategies, supporting concepts and structural relationships implicit in MYCIN's empirical rules (i.e. hypothesis–data links), it becomes easier to support such roles.

Knowledge analysis has been applied in two main ways: to the analysis of expert systems of a particular type, and as a tool in knowledge acquisition.

(1) *Analysis of expert systems*

On the basis of detailed analyses, both Bennett (1985) and Clancey (1984) concluded that most existing diagnostic systems employ essentially the same small set of basic elements and relations. In other words, while reasoning and search strategies were found to vary considerably between systems, the basic knowledge elements and inference structure were not. Bennett (1985) exploited this commonality in the development of ROGET, an automated knowledge acquisition tool. This system helps elicit from a domain expert the "conceptual structure" for a diagnostic system in a new sub-domain. ROGET is equipped with the general structure and knowledge elements that make up a typical MYCIN-like diagnostic system. The domain expert is able to tailor this structure in accordance with the unique features of a particular domain. Basic elements in the diagnostic domain include "findings", "symptoms" and "hypotheses", arranged in the same kind of inference structure across subdomains. Other expert domains would appear amenable to a similar treatment (Wielinga and Breuker, 1984). Clancey's (1984, 1985) influential analysis of expert systems has already been referred to (see Section 3.1.1).

(2) *Knowledge acquisition tool*

Some of the ideas already discussed are incorporated in a framework for knowledge acquisition proposed by Wielinga and Breuker (1984). Their approach centres on the use of *interpretation models*. An interpretation model consists of a classification of canonical elements, structuring relations, strategies and a representation of the inference structure for a class of domains. An analysis of the task the expert has to perform can form the initial basis of a model. Once formulated, it provides a set of abstract categories and expectancies which help direct the gathering of data (from textbooks, interviews, verbal protocols, etc.) and its subsequent interpretation. Because an interpretation model is formalized at an epistemological level, the knowledge engineer is forced to analyse the data at this level in order to test and refine the model. Some early results using this approach in a variety of domains appear quite promising (e.g. HaKong and Hickman, 1985; Wielinga and Breuker, 1984). However, Breuker and Wielinga (1984) point out that not all constructable interpretation models are implementable using existing AI techniques.

Considered as a strategy for emulating expert cognition in a given domain, the knowledge analysis approach has a number of limitations:

● Fidelity to domain-specific features of processing (as opposed to knowledge organization) tends to be regarded as a secondary issue.

● Epistemological analysis is concerned with making explicit the types of knowledge that *may* exist in a particular domain — not with faithfully representing what individual experts actually know.

● Epistemological analysis can make explicit types of knowledge that are represented in expert cognition only in a highly procedur- alized, highly inaccessible form. That is, for the expert such explicated knowledge may not in fact exist.

In summary, knowledge analysis is a useful technique in its own right. As an approach to emulating domain expertise it offers a valuable perspective, but not a complete solution.

5.4   EMULATING EXPERT COGNITION

5.4.1   Introduction

In the two previous sections we have considered approaches to cognitive emulation centred on the individual expert and domain expertise respectively. Individual differences in expert thinking provide the psychological justification for the first approach; the domain-adapted nature of human expertise the justification for the second. However, a psychological rationale can also be found for an approach to expert system design centred on general considerations of expert cognitive functioning. Put another way, across many specialist domains the cognitive changes that accompany the deve- lopment of expertise are broadly similar (see Chapter 2, especially Table 2.1). None of the research reviewed below attempts to embody all — or even a majority — of the cognitive features listed in Table 2.1. Instead, these studies concentrate on modelling selective aspects of expert reasoning and knowledge organization, in accordance with the knowledge engineering objectives of the researchers involved. [It is important to bear in mind that any implementation at this level also requires instantiating with regard to a particular domain — and possibly at the individual expert level also.]

Two broad perspectives on emulating general expert cognition can be distinguished. The first is concerned with modelling dynamic aspects of expert thinking: i.e. how knowledge structures and reason- ing strategies change as experience is acquired, and the dynamic aspects of expert problem solving. The second category of research is directed towards emulating particular cognitive functions; for exam- ple, tuition, critiquing or guidance. As we shall see, both areas are now being actively investigated.

5.4.2   Emulating the dynamics of expert cognition

Recent cognitive research (e.g. Johnson *et al.*, 1981; Feltovich *et al.*, 1984; see also Chapter 2) has drawn attention to the role of experience in the development of human expertise. However, the dynamic changes in expert reasoning and knowledge organization that result from experience is not reflected in the current generation of expert systems. Here we shall review attempts to supply expert systems with such dynamic capabilities.

One line of approach (e.g. Kolodner, 1984; Riesbeck, 1984; Schank and Slade, 1984) builds on AI research into episodic memory and natural language processing initiated by Schank (e.g. Schank, 1982). Central to this research — and the expert system applications — are the concepts of "semantic memory", "episodic memory", "memory organization packages (MOPs)", "similarity-based generalization" and "failure-driven learning". Because these concepts may be unfamiliar, they are introduced below, before an examination of their (proposed) application in knowledge engineering.

To begin with then, a distinction has been made between semantic memory and episodic memory (one incidently, that was first made in cognitive psychology):

Semantic Memory Human semantic memory is the memory for facts we know, arranged in some kind of hierarchical network (Kolodner, 1984). For example, in a semantic memory "stool" may be defined as a type of "chair", in turn defined as an instance of "furniture". Properties and relations are handled within the overall hierarchical framework. In terms of human expertise, semantic memory represents the store of factual knowledge that a novice acquires. But experience is required to convert facts into usable expert knowledge (Kolodner, 1984).

Episodic Memory If semantic memory encodes facts, then episodic memory encodes experience. An episode is a record of an experienced event like visiting a restaurant or a diagnostic consultation. Generalized episodes are also created, representing typical events. Information in episodic memory is defined and organized in accordance with its intended uses in different situations or operations. On this view it is the development of extensive and highly tuned episodic memory that above all else distinguishes the domain expert from the novice (e.g. Kolodner, 1984). That is, even assuming that factual knowledge (semantic memory) remains constant as expertise develops, the expert possesses better episodic definitions for using it.

Episodes are implemented as MOPs:

Memory Organisation Packets (MOPs) MOPs are a knowledge representation formalism developed by Schank (e.g. 1982) for implementing episodes. They are modular frame-like structures that serve to organize, index and cross-reference an episodic memory of events. MOPs are organized in a generalization hierarchy: each MOP can have several other MOPs as sub-parts, and each sub-part can participate in several higher-level MOPs. [The MOP formalism evolved from Schank's (Schank and Abelson, 1977) earlier notion of a script — a formalism in which each event is represented in a single large frame-like unit. This reformulation was prompted partly by empirical tests of the script concept in psychology, and partly for efficiency reasons.]

Two forms of experience-based learning are identified in the development of episodic memory — similarity-based generalization and failure-driven learning:

Similarity-based Generalization When similarities are detected between already-established concepts in episodic memory — what Schank (1982) calls "reminding" — these similarities are extracted to form a generalized episode. Thus two or three diagnostic consultations with patients may be sufficient for a clinician to encode a generalized episode about typical features of this situation. Thereafter, individual episodes need only record their distinguishing features: gain, this results in economical storage. Generalized MOPs are also useful in interpreting and reasoning about newly encountered events, which are understood as instances of existing generalized episodes.

Failure-driven learning In performing cognitive tasks, people are often aware of strategy failures, exceptional events, etc. According to Schank (1982) and others, this awareness triggers failure-driven learning; a process which involves:

● detecting the failure
● attempting to allocate blame ("explain") the failure — the explanation serves as an index to the failed episode
● when a similar situation is encountered later it is referred to the failed episode via this index
● if a solution was found to the initial failure, the same solution can be applied to the second situation; otherwise, the two episodes can be compared to determine the cause of their joint failure, and the process of indexing and referral repeated

Kolodner (e.g. 1984), in particular, has shown how these concepts can be applied to understanding the development of human expertise in a single domain (psychiatry). Her work is based on the verbal protocols of doctors making psychiatric diagnoses and recommending treatment. An elaboration of the MOP idea is used to represent the doctors' experiences: Process MOPs are an explicit representation of the reasoning strategies of the diagnostician; while Diagnostic MOPs represent domain-specific diagnostic knowledge. Developments of the two types of MOP are highly co-ordinated. The theory is partially implemented in a computer program called SHRINK. Riesbeck (1984) employs the same basic concepts of failure-driven learning and MOPs to model the development of expertise in economic reasoning — again with a partial computer implementation.

On this view of human expertise, today's expert systems suffer from two main deficiencies:

(1) Unlike human experts, most expert systems were never novices — starting out with one type of knowledge base and ending up with another (Riesbeck, 1984).
(2) Current expert systems do not have a memory — the same case will be treated in the same way, however often it is encountered (Schank, 1982). The human ability to use and learn from experience is missing.

Kolodner (1984), Riesbeck (1984) and others (e.g. Schank and Slade, 1984) take a similar view on what this characterization of human expertise implies for expert system design. First of all, the program should be supplied with the kind of factual knowledge that a domain novice can acquire from textbooks and other public sources. In addition, the initial program will require rules for reorganizing its knowledge base and reasoning strategies as new experiences are encountered. Then the program can be given a set of experiences (e.g. cases to diagnose), plus feedback on its performance. Modelling how experience changes the way an expert reasons like this is seen as the most effective method for equipping an expert system with the capabilities of human experts.

Kolodner (1984) herself points out the main problems with this approach:

● it is highly complex (cf. rule-based systems) and consequently difficult to implement
● verifying that expert reasoning and knowledge organization change as predicted by the model is a nontrivial task
● explanation of the system's reasoning presents a major challenge

A further difficulty relates to the psychological validity of the underlying model of human expertise and how it develops. In particular, although concepts such as semantic memory, episodic memory, etc. are familiar ones in cognitive psychology, it has not yet been shown how the model can account for the empirical literature on expert-novice differences (see Chapter 2).

The "competent expert systems" methodology (Keravnou and Johnson, 1986) is also concerned with dynamic aspects of expert thinking. Here, however, interest is in how dynamic aspects of expert strategy execution can be modelled in an explicit and principled way. A "competent" expert system is one that represents explicitly the reasoning strategies and domain knowledge structures adopted by experts in a particular domain — i.e. the "model of competence" of the domain . The methodology specifies tools for eliciting models of competence, and mapping them into knowledge representation schemes. During knowledge acquisition the dynamics of how strategic knowledge is used are analysed: i.e. how it is decomposed and integrated, how strategies are selected in context, etc.

Keravnou and Johnson (1986) make strong claims for this methodology, including enhanced system-user dialogues and explanations, improved knowledge acquisition, and greater power and flexibility in problem solving. From the standpoint of cognitive emulation, the main criticism is that "competent" expert systems are likely to lack plausibility as psychological models. That is, the emphasis on explicit representation, and on a clear separation of strategic and domain knowledge, is at odds with the highly compiled nature of human expertise (see Chapter 2).

5.4.3   Emulating the cognitive functions experts perform

The approaches to cognitive emulation reviewed in the previous section were selective in their emphasis on the dynamic aspects of expert cognition. Here we concentrate on recent attempts to emulate another aspect of human expertise — the ability of experts to perform a variety of cognitive functions. Early research efforts focused on developing expert systems to perform the role of problem solvers. That is to say, programs like DENDRAL, MYCIN and XCON were all principally designed to produce technically correct solutions to well-defined problems. And most of the research on cognitive emulation reviewed so far in this book has been directed at modelling the problem-solving skills of human experts. Clinical diagnostic skills are the most frequently cited example.

A combination of factors has prompted the recent shift in research interest to include other cognitive functions. Important among these are :

(1) User dissatisfaction with the problem-solving paradigm. In this paradigm the user acts as a data source, supplying information to the program through a system-controlled dialogue. This sequence ends with the system supplying a completed solution which the user may either accept or reject. The problem-solving paradigm arises from a technology-driven approach to expert system design in which the user has little scope for exercising personal control or responsibility (Woods, 1986). As such, the often reported problem of "user acceptance" in knowledge engineering may result primarily from expert systems performing inappropriate and unacceptable cognitive roles (e.g. Coombs and Alty, 1984; Woods, 1986).

(2) Detailed observational studies of what experts really do (e.g. Coombs and Alty, 1984; Kidd, 1985c) are beginning to reveal the wide range of cognitive functions experts actually perform. A basic finding is that users normally play a more active role when consulting an expert than present expert systems allow. For example, users may help define the problem to be solved, suppy a set of constraints that any solution must satisfy, or formulate their own plan for the expert to critique. Expert systems designed to support such co-operative problem solving activity appear far more acceptable to users (Coombs and Alty, 1984; Kidd, 1985c; Langlotz and Shortliffe, 1984).

The particular cognitive functions to be considered here are critiquing, guidance, remedy negotiation and tuition:

(1) *Critiquing*
A critique is an explanation of important differences between a user's proposed solution (or plan, etc.) and the solution the expert would have proposed. Initially, the critiquing function was thought to occur principally where the user is either a domain expert (e.g. Langlotz and Shortliffe, 1984) or a full or partial expert in an overlapping domain of expertise (Coombs and Alty, 1984). But analyses of naturally occurring dialogues between experts and novice users (Kidd, 1985c) make it clear that critiquing of user proposals takes place across a wide spectrum of user skill.

Among expert systems that embody a critiquing function are :

● ATTENDING a program for critiquing anaesthetic management (Miller, 1984)
● ONCOCIN critiques the therapy plans of physicians for treating cancer patients (Langlotz and Shortliffe, 1984)

Critiquing can take a variety of forms : e.g. warning of prerequisite violations, reports on possible consequences and side effects, reminders of potentially relevant information. Thus expert systems designed to perform a critiquing function are able to adopt a less intrusive, "silent partner" role. In the case of ONCOCIN, for example, the system analyses the problem and develops a therapy plan for itself, but only makes this known if the plan entered by the physician differs in significant respects. As a consequence, the user is not interrupted in a majority of cases. Langlotz and Shortliffe (1984) adapted ONCOCIN to perform a critiquing role in response to user dissatisfaction with its original problem solving orientation. No apparent attempt was made to emulate expert cognition in the implementation of ONCOCIN, which relies on sophisticated AI techniques.

(2) *Guidance*

In an advanced technological society expertise becomes fragmented and highly specialized. As a consequence the solution to many technical problems can require the co-ordinated efforts of several specialists. Experts in one domain are often called upon to help experts in overlapping fields to extend and refine their understanding at the interface of their two domains of knowledge (Coombs and Alty, 1984). This guidance function relies more on educational than problem solving skills.

In order to implement a prototype guidance system, Coombs and Alty (1984) concluded that:

> it is necessary to isolate the fundamental cognitive procedure underlying interactions. To do this systematically requires some theory of the role of conceptualization and understanding in problem solving (p. 139)

The authors considered cognitive theories from psychology and AI, but found them insufficiently developed for application purposes. Instead, Coombs and Alty based their program on a general theory of cognition developed in cybernetics by Pask (e.g. Pask, 1975). Pask's Conversation Theory is too complex to elaborate here, but it basically attempts to establish the minimum theoretical structures needed to support different cognitive processes. Coombs and Alty found it a useful framework within which to model the guidance function. The implemented system, MINDPAD, helps users in the task of debugging simple PROLOG programs. It supports the user's problem solving efforts through making available resources, suggesting tasks, and critiquing user explanations.

(3) *Remedy negotiation*

Diagnostic expert systems provide answers to two main questions: (a) what is at fault? and (b) what is the appropriate remedy? However, these do not appear representative of the questions users actually put to experts. A study of naturally-occurring consultations in several diagnostic domains by Kidd (1985c) reveals a rather different picture. In contrast to current expert systems (that output a take-it-or-leave-it solution at the end of a consultation), a complex process of remedy negotation between expert and user was observed. This can involve:

- the expert proposing a tentative remedy early in the dialogue
- the user volunteering constraints (e.g. "it must be fast") on potential remedies
- the user rejecting a remedy because it has already been tried and failed, or does not meet user-imposed constraints.
- the expert critiquing remedies proposed by the user
- the expert explaining why a remedy worked, or trying to convince a user to adopt a particular remedy.

Kidd (1985c) considers the implications of these findings for the design of diagnostic advice systems. She rightly points out that present AI technology cannot support the sophisticated mixed-initiative dialogues, etc. needed to emulate properly the expert's role in this context. Instead, Kidd considers how AI works on the representation of, and reasoning about, deeper level structural and functional knowledge (e.g. Davis, 1984) can be adapted to support a remedy negotiation role. This AI work overlaps with cognitive research into the mental models of human experts (see Chapter 2).

(4) *Tutoring*

Like guidance, tutoring is a cognitive function which requires educational skills (as much as problem solving ability) from an expert. One major expert system to support a tutoring role is NEOMYCIN (Clancey and Letsinger, 1981; Hasling, Clancey and Rennels, 1984). More specifically, NEOMYCIN is a consultation program with a knowledge base configured so as to promote understanding about the diagnostic strategies employed in a particular medical domain. The basic assumption is that for "understanders" to be able to solve domain problems for themselves, they need — in addition to domain knowledge — some idea of the problem-solving process. To this end, the approach adopted in NEOMYCIN is to model human reasoning, with diagnostic procedures represented explicitly. [The model includes a working memory of activated hypotheses, forward-chain-

ing in response to clinical data, and hypotheses triggered by associa-
tion. Some empirical support for such a model of clinical cognition is
provided in a study by Patel and Groen (1986).] So, rather than
having expert diagnostic knowledge implicitly embedded in the
control program's code (cf. MYCIN), it is expressed explicitly in the
knowledge base as meta-rules.

In short, NEOMYCIN supports a tutoring function using an
explicit model of diagnostic reasoning. However, while this may be
an effective approach to teaching expertise, it probably does not
emulate the cognitive mechanisms involved in human expert tuition.
For, as was noted in Chapter 2, experts are often completely unaware
of their own problem solving processes.

In this section we have looked at programs designed to support
cognitive functions beyond the simple problem solving of most earlier
systems. The researchers involved differ greatly in their attempts to
emulate the cognitive processes underlying the performance of a
particular role. Thus, at one extreme, Langlotz and Shortliffe (1984)
were able to develop a critiquing system using standard AI techniques. At the other, Coombs and Alty (1984) employed a well-
articulated theory of cognition to implement a prototype guidance
system. The decision to adopt an emulation strategy in such cases
appears to reflect two principal considerations:

(a) When it is possible to build a program to perform an expert
    function using formal AI methods there is little point in experi-
    menting with cognitive models.
(b) The available cognitive models must be sufficiently robust and
    powerful to support an implemented program.

5.5 EMULATING USER COGNITION

5.5.1 Introduction

The previous three sections of this chapter have considered
approaches to the emulation of *expert* cognition. But for many
researchers (e.g. Breuker and Wielinga, 1983b; Fox, 1983; Kidd,
1985a; Sleeman, 1984) it has seemed at least as important to achieve
compatibility at the cognitive level between an expert system and the
user. A good match between system and user is seen as vital for
several reasons:

● without this cognitive compatability the system's behaviour can
   appear surprising and unnatural to the user
● to counter the potential dehumanizing influence of expert systems

technology (through ensuring the knowledge and reasoning of the system are understandable to the user, user-controlled dialogues, etc.)
● to ensure the system will be accepted within its intended social and organizational context of use

User interface design is acknowledged as an important issue in present generation systems. However, while a substantial amount of development effort and application code often goes into constructing "user friendly" interfaces, work on tailoring expert systems to match user cognition at a deeper level is still largely at the research stage. Some of this research is seeking to make expert systems more usable by designing them so that they process information in the way users process information (Fox, 1983). The emulation of "human information processing" is the subject of the next section (5.6). Here we focus on how expert systems can be adapted to model the requirements of particular users, or types of user.

Two common uses of the term "user model" in the expert system literature need to be distinguished at the outset. First, it can refer to the representation an expert system may have of the system's intended end user. Second, there is the human user's conceptual model — or, as seems more likely, plurality of models (e.g. Hammond and Barnard, 1985, Young, 1981) of the specialist domain, the task to be performed, and the computer system itself. We are mainly concerned with the first sense of the term here.

5.5.2   The benefits of user models
Sparck Jones (1985) identifies three main benefits that the possession of user models can confer on expert systems:

(1) *Acceptability*. To be acceptable the form in which information is elicited and explanations given need to be tailored to the intended user — be they novice or super-expert.
(2) *Efficiency of system operations*. For example, the most efficient mode of system-user interaction will usually vary according to the user's level of skill.
(3) *Effectiveness*. User models can facilitate more effective task performance through more accurate interpretation of user behaviour, and by making the system's requirements more comprehensible to a particular user.

5.5.3   User characteristics in user models
Many types of expert system are possible. For some of these a representation of the user would serve little useful purpose — for

example, autonomous problem solving systems where there is minimal user involvement. More often, though, expert systems act as some kind of "knowledgeable assistant" (Kidd, 1985a) to the user. Where this is the case, an expert system might benefit from the inclusion of several types of knowledge about the user. Specifically, about the user's:

● conceptualization of the task domain
● way of formulating problems
● goals, needs, assumptions, expectations
● model of how the system works
● typical errors and misconceptions
● level of competence
● preferred method of interacting with the system
● acceptance criteria
● the user's role.

5.5.4   User modelling techniques

Breuker and Wielinga (1983b) include a stage of "User analysis" as part of their knowledge engineering methodology. They argue for the use of several methods — interviews, experiments, simulation, protocols of real-life interactions, etc. — in order to elicit the kinds of user information listed above.

Many of the current AI techniques for representing user attributes were developed by researchers working on intelligent tutoring systems (see e.g. Sleeman and Brown, 1982). One classification of user models (e.g. Sleeman, 1984) distinguishes:

(1) *Scalar models* The level of expertise of the user is expressed as a single number. For example, in the KEYSTROKE model of Card, Moran and Newell (1983), the number of keystrokes is used as a measure of text-editing skill.
(2) *Ad hoc modelling systems* These exploit the specific features of the underlying system, such as how the inference engine works.
(3) *Profile models* The user is represented by a set of weighted attributes (e.g. "romantic"), which enables the system to match the user to, say, a suitable book or film.
(4) *Overlay models* The competence of the user–novice is represented as a subset of the expert's. So, for example, if the expert's knowledge is expressed as a semantic network, the novice's knowledge "overlays" a part of this network.
(5) *Process models* A representation of the user's problem solving processes. For example, student's incorrect, or "buggy" arith-

metic procedures were modelled in BUGGY (Brown and Burton, 1978).

It is only with the last modelling technique, process models, that a serious attempt at cognitive emulation is made. The other types of model are more directed to representing *what* a user knows, expects, etc.; rather than the *how* question addressed by process models. Unlike *ad hoc* models, process models are executable using standard inference engines (Sleeman, 1984). So, in principle at least, this emulation technique could be adopted more widely than it currently is.

Where the intended user group is homogeneous, the entire expert system can be designed in accordance with the characteristics of that group. In contrast, heterogeneity in the proposed users may require that several *a priori* user models about the different types of user are built into the system. The problem is then one of selecting/tailoring a model to a particular user at run-time. A number of ways of inferring a suitable user model have been developed:

● the system takes the initiative and questions the user
● the system infers the user's characteristics from their behaviour
● the system is told to expect a user of a certain type, perhaps by setting a parameter

The appropriate mode of system–user dialogue (e.g. linear command syntax, menus, natural language, graphical displays, etc.) can be selected using the same basic methods (Bundy, 1984).

5.5.5   Expert system applications
Some notable applications of user modelling techniques in expert systems include:

(1) In a medical system developed by Wallis and Shortliffe (1982), difficulty level is expressed as an integer. The concepts used by the system to explain its reasoning varies according to the difficulty level selected by the user.
(2) The Interviewer/Reasoner model (Gerring, Shortliffe and van Melle, 1982) — as the name implies — consists of two main parts. The "Reasoner" is a rule-based AI program which does most of the computation; the "Interviewer" is a user-oriented display program that mediates between the user and the system.
(3) Intelligent Front Ends (IFEs). This type of expert system acts as a friendly interface to a software package that would otherwise be incomprehensible to many potential users (Bundy, 1984). IFEs

use AI techniques to enable the user to communicate with the underlying package using their own terminology. Through a user-oriented dialogue a model of the user's problem is constructed, and translated into a form the package understands.

(4) UMFE (Sleeman, 1984) is a user modelling front-end sub-system which tailors its explanations to the user's level of understanding. Concepts used by the back-end expert system are graded by UMFE according to difficulty. Depending on the user's response to initial concepts, UMFE is able to infer additional concepts the user may/may not find comprehensible.

5.5.6 Problems in user emulation

The requirements of effective user modelling are often beyond the scope of existing AI techniques to deliver:

(1) *Ambiguities in user modelling*

Sparck Jones (1985) observes that a simple one-to-one match between a given user and user model could be impossible to establish in certain expert system applications. In medical advisory systems, for example, it is necessary to distinguish between the patient and doctor (system user) as separate people, and possibly between the different roles a single user performs. Thus user emulation can require manipulating a multiplicity of user models with different functions and different bases. Moveover, the system's knowledge of a user may need to be dynamic — responding to changes in the user's understanding, skill, etc. as they occur (Sparck Jones, 1985).

(2) *False expectations*

Sophisticated user-oriented dialogues (e.g. natural language interfaces) and other user modelling techniques can give the user a misleading impression of an expert system's capabilities. Where the intelligence exhibited by the user interface is unmatched by the performance of the underlying system, there is a danger that the user will place an unjustified reliance on the system's decisions (Boden, 1985). Boden suggests that the system should "flag" its limitations to the user in these circumstances.

(3) *Implications for the underlying system*

According to Sparck Jones (1985), user modelling cannot be effective unless the modelling component has proper access to the knowledge and operations of the "back-end" system. The provision of a non-trivial natural language capability may require an equally close coupling between interface and back-end sub-systems (Sparck Jones, 1984).

(4) *Representational complexity*

It is unlikely that all the user's knowledge about the problem domain, about the task to be performed, and about the computer system can be integrated into a unitary user model (Hammond and Barnard, 1985). For instance, Young (1981) found that users' knowledge of pocket calculator usage fell into two distinct types. On the one hand, he describes "task-action mapping rules" — a set of rules/procedures for reaching certain task goals. These are complemented by "conceptual models" representing knowledge about the relations between system entities. [These models often have an analogical basis, e.g. the "Typewriter" model used in word processing (Hammond and Barnard, 1985)]. Moreover, as the tasks tackled by expert systems become more open-ended and complex, multiple knowledge representations will become increasingly necessary to capture the user's knowledge (Sleeman, 1984).

(5) *Conflicting demands*

A basic conflict can arise between the user modelling and task performance components of a system: the former requires responsiveness to the user, while the latter is computationally-oriented. Gerring *et al.*'s (1982) Interviewer/Reasoner model addresses this issue by implementing these components as separate (though interacting) programs. A similar rationale underlies the notion of Intelligent Front Ends to complex software packages (Bundy, 1984).

More important here, emulating the user may conflict with emulating expert reasoning. For as Kiss (reported by Fox, 1983) points out, although emulating user cognition may improve intelligibility, it can also lead to systems which lack power and which fail to complement human processing methods. In view of the contrasting benefits available from emulating experts and user, techniques are required to enable both forms of emulation to co-exist within a single system. A system architecture in which user and expert cognition are modelled in separate components, along the lines suggested above, offers one potential solution. We shall return to this and related issues in the discussion (Section 5.8).

5.6 EMULATING HUMAN INFORMATION PROCESSING

5.6.1 Introduction

Invoking the principle of cognitive emulation at this level (see Fig. 5.1) implies one, or both, of the following:

● Seeking compatibility between the architecture of expert systems

and the architecture of human information processing (cf. Fox, 1983)
- expert system work directly inspired by research in cognitive psychology: i.e. specific findings, models and hypotheses.

Expert systems adopting this approach are analogous to the "representative programs" developed by cognitive scientists. Representative programs attempt to embody general mechanisms of human thinking without simulating any individual person. They thus perform a role in cognitive science comparable to that of the "representative firm" in economics (Simon, 1979).

The discussion of cognitive emulation at this level centres on five key issues:

(1) The extent to which the standard three-element system architecture of expert systems corresponds to the architecture of human cognition.
(2) The psychological plausibility of particular knowledge representation formalisms and system architectures.
(3) Attempts to make expert systems compatible with the limitations of human information processing.
(4) The explicit representation of knowledge.
(5) Approaches to the handling of uncertainty in expert systems inspired by cognitive psychology.

5.6.2   The architecture of expert systems and human cognition

(1) *Structural comparisons*
There is a basic similarity in the system architecture of, on the one hand, performance-oriented expert systems and, on the other, computer simulations of human cognition developed by cognitive scientists. In both types of program it is frequently possible to distinguish three fundamental architectural components:

(a) A static store of permanent knowledge represented in some explicit form, e.g. production rules, frames.
(b) A dynamic store for holding temporary data.
(c) A processing element which uses the knowledge in (a) to make inferences based on (b).

As noted in Chapter 2, in the context of applied expert systems the names given are typically (a) knowledge base, (b) dynamic database, and (c) inference engine; while in cognitive science these elements more often translate as (a) long-term memory, (b) working (or short-term) memory and (c) cognitive processor. This correspondance is illustrated in Fig. 5.2 and Fig. 5.3 respectively.

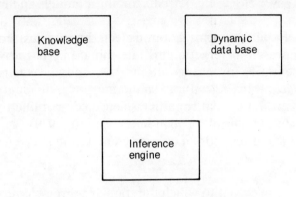

Fig. 5.2 — Expert system architecture.

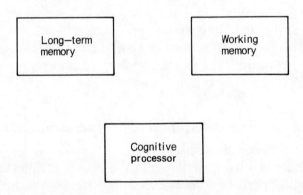

Fig. 5.3 — Human cognitive architecture shown as comprising three independent elements.

Why research in these two areas should have converged on the same basic system architecture is open to various interpretations (e.g. Davis and King, 1977; Hayes-Roth, Waterman and Lenat, 1978). Hayes-Roth *et al.* (1978) make the point that the two areas offer nearly complementary theories of information processing, with cognitive psychology focusing on problems of knowledge acquisition, retrieval and storage, and AI/expert systems on issues of knowledge representation and utilization.

On one interpretation, the correspondence between Figs. 5.2 and

5.3 could be taken as evidence that current expert systems emulate human cognition in a fundamental respect. But this would represent an over-simplification of the more complex picture uncovered by cognitive research. In particular, the modularity of the three structural elements implied in Fig 5.3 is called into question by some empirical findings. A few selected examples from the cognitive literature will serve to illustrate this apparent non-modularity:

Long-term memory/working memory
The concept of working memory has gone through many transformations in the psychological literature. In earlier accounts it was seen essentially as a uniform, limited-capacity and separate store for the storage and processing of short-term information (see e.g. Newell and Simon, 1972). But this view has become increasingly superseded by more complex formulations in which, for example, working memory is defined as the currently "activated" portion of long-term memory (e.g. Anderson, 1983a; Card *et al.*, 1983). Indeed, Card *et al.* (1983) represent the relation between the two types of memory as shown in Fig. 5.4, with working memory nested within long-term memory.

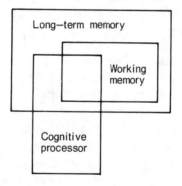

Fig. 5.4 — Human cognitive architecture shown as comprising three overlapping elements.

Working memory/cognitive processor
Studies of individuals with highly skilled memories led Chase and Ericsson (1982) to propose a model of working memory that includes rapid-accessing retrieval mechanisms to long-term memory. On this view, there is an intimate connection between working memory and attentional processes. Baddeley (1981) has reached a similar conclu-

sion. In his account — based on a mature research programme — working memory is partitioned into three sub-stores; one of which (the "Central Executive") is assumed to have a limited amount of processing capacity of its own.

Cognitive processor/long-term memory
The acquisition of cognitive skill and expertise is accompanied by the proceduralization of knowledge (see Chapter 2). And there is plenty of evidence for the importance of procedurally represented knowledge in human cognition generally (e.g. Elio, 1986; Norman and Rumelhart, 1981). While it is possible to model procedural knowledge using some kind of declarative formalism — production rules, say — there remains a strong likelihood that human procedural knowledge is held in a highly compiled and contextually dependent form: with control and knowledge packaged closely together.

On the basis of findings such as these, one could argue that Fig. 5.4 offers a more accurate diagrammatic representation of how long-term memory, working memory and cognitive processes are related than Fig. 5.3. However, the modularity of cognitive architecture implied by Fig. 5.3 is less contentious if viewed as a simplifying assumption necessary in cognitive modelling. While this clearly weakens the claim that the system architecture of standard expert systems emulates the human cognitive architecture, a certain structural similarity remains.

(2) Formal comparisons
It is informative to compare performance-oriented expert systems with cognitive simulations from a formal as well as a structural viewpoint. In particular, there are some notable differences in the formal properties of production systems adapted for either purpose (Davis and King, 1977; Hayes-Roth et al., 1978; Young, 1979). The early, "pure" production systems used to model human problem solving, perception, etc. (e.g. Newell and Simon, 1972; Newell, 1973) were characterized by:

- a single-level rule base (long-term memory)
- constrained rule format (e.g. no negation, disjunctive conditions, or nesting of conditions permitted)
- simple pattern matching capabilities (e.g. variable substitution, but no evaluation of complex predicates)
- syntactic conflict resolution (e.g. based on rule of the specificity of conditions)
- condition driven control (i.e. forward-chaining) using a linear cycle of recognize–act cycles

● size-limited working memory

These features represent a set of purity and simplicity restrictions adopted to capture the invariants of human cognition (Hayes-Roth *et al*., 1978; Young, 1979). The constraints placed on rule format, for instance, enable a stronger analogy to be drawn with psychological stimulus-response behaviours than would otherwise be possible. At its strictest, this amounts to a highly principled approach to cognitive modelling; one in which every aspect of the system is assumed to have a psychological correlate (Davis and King, 1977).

The main cost is loss of computational power — not usually a critical problem in cognitive modelling, but a serious drawback in performance-oriented expert systems. This helps explain why many of the purity restrictions are relaxed in applied systems to allow, for example:

● additional types of knowledge representation (including semantic nets, frames, procedural attachment)
● probabilistic measures of uncertainty attached to rules
● backward-chaining and bi-directional control structures
● specialized and multi-layered working memories (e.g. blackboards)
● meta-rules that control the invocation of object rules
● partial matching between working memory elements and rule conditions (or consequents in backward-chaining systems)
● knowledge in different states of activation (e.g. quiescent, semi-active, fully active)
● no limit on the number of symbols created and maintained in working memory for pattern matching

Interestingly, many of these relaxations have started to appear in more recent cognitive simulations. This point is very well illustrated by one major attempt to model the human cognitive architecture: developed by Anderson (1983a). While ACT* retains an overall production system architecture it includes, alongside the standard production rule memory:

● a long-term declarative memory expressed in a network representation
● analogical(spatial) representations
● a working memory consisting of currently activated knowledge in long-term memory, and thus of variable size
● a pattern matching mechanism capable of partial matching and sensitive to probabilistic criteria

This is not an isolated example. Another is a cognitive model of human planning behaviour (Hayes-Roth and Hayes-Roth, 1979). This well illustrates the relaxation on working memory uniformity, since the model employs a blackboard architecture with multiple, multi-layered working memories (i.e. blackboards). In general, the belief that a single, simple system architecture or knowledge formalism is sufficient to capture all human cognitive functioning — or even a substantial part of it — is no longer widely subscribed to in cognitive psychology.

The willingness of cognitive modellers to adopt a wider range of AI techniques serves to blur the distinction between knowledge engineering and cognitive science. A continuation of the convergence between the two fields would provide a compelling argument for the cognitive emulation principle. Research developments in the near future should make it clear whether the architectural requirements of applied expert systems and cognitive models coincide fundamentally or not.

It may turn out that the cognitive scientist's more principled approach to program design is the limiting factor on this process of convergence. For whereas the expert system builder is entitled to use all the programming devices at his or her disposal, the cognitive scientist must — in principle, at least — be able to justify program features on theoretical grounds. While this stricture has discouraged *ad hoc* program fixes ("kludges") in simulation programs, it has not prevented psychological validity being claimed for a wide variety of system architectures and knowledge formalisms. It is these claims that we shall now consider.

5.6.3 Psychological validity of different system architectures and knowledge representation formalisms

AI researchers have developed a large number of system architectures and knowledge formalisms (see e.g. Barr and Feigenbaum, 1981; or Rumelhart and Norman, 1983). Some of these have been advanced as general models of human information processing, such as production systems (Newell and Simon, 1972) and the blackboard architecture (Hayes-Roth, 1983). More often though, an individual architecture or formalism is adopted because it appears well-adapted to modelling a particular cognitive function. Table 5.3 illustrates the different areas of research various architectures/formalisms have found special favour in. Cognitive scientists justify these choices on theoretical grounds, but also in terms of sufficiency (Young, 1979). In other words, because so little is known about human cognition, a

Table 5.3 — Research areas in cognitive science in which selected system architectures and knowledge representations are typically adopted

Representation/ architecture	Research area	Sample reference
Production Systems	Problem Solving Perceptual Processes Skill Acquisition	Newell and Simon (1972) Newell (1973) Anderson (1983a)
Semantic Networks	Long-term Memory	Anderson and Bower (1973)
Schema-based Formalisms (frames, scripts, MOPs)	Text Understanding Memory for Episodes	Schank and Abelson (1977) Schank (1982)
Spatial Representations	Imagery Vision	Kosslyn (1980) Marr (1982)
Blackboard Model	Reading Planning	McClelland and Rumelhart (1981) Hayes-Roth and Hayes-Roth (1979)

successful simulation program has some claim to psychological validity solely on the grounds that it works.

Many cognitive scientists (e.g. Anderson, 1983a; Rumelhart and Norman, 1983; Sloman, 1984) now take seriously the hypothesis that human thinking is a multi-representational system — one that may parallel the range of representations used in psychological modelling. On this view, each aspect of the represented world is mapped into the representation best suited to a particular use.

Table 5.4 makes the point that variants on all the architectures/

Table 5.4 — Examples of expert system research employing different system architectures and knowledge representations

Representation/ architecture	System name	Application area	Reference
Production Systems	MYCIN	Medicine	Shortliffe (1976)
Semantic Networks	PROSPECTOR	Geology	Duda et al. (1979)
Frames	PIP	Medicine	Pauker et al. (1976)
Spatial Representations	ACRONYM	Image understanding	Brooks (1983)
Blackboard Model	JOBBES	Job selection	Boyle (1985)

formalisms included in Table 5.3 have also found employment in expert systems research. It is thus not possible at present to assess the psychological validity of an expert system simply by whether it employs a particular architecture/formalism or not. Instead, the question of psychological validity needs to be addressed on a more contextual basis. One might ask, for example:

● does the selected architecture/formalism perform the designated task adequately? (i.e. is it *sufficient*?)
● is the architecture/formalism selected based on a psychological considerations? Is it being used in a principled way?
● is the architecture/formalism selected representative of those used by cognitive scientists to model human performance on comparable tasks?

5.6.4 Limitations on human information processing

Human information processing capacity is limited (see Chapter 2). This has led to several suggestions as to how expert systems might be adapted to reflect these limitations. To consider a few:

Fox, Alvey and Myers (1983) discuss the need for a "low-demand" expert system package to cater for situations where the computer may only be one of a number of activities. So, for example, it is unrealistic to assume that in routine clinical practice, with a patient present perhaps, a doctor's activities will be centred around the computer. [This is an assumption often made in MMI research.] What is required under such conditions, suggest Fox *et al.*, (1983), is a system which makes minimal demands on the user. The authors describe PROPS, a prototype expert system package human-engineered to facilite speedy querying and user control of the system.

A comparable problem can arise in real-time process control applications. For instance, Paterson, Sachs and Turner (1985) point out that operators at one particular gas development installation have access to around 35 000 items of data. These authors suggest the need for an expert system to reduce the problem of cognitive overload that can arise where operators are faced with large amounts of rapidly changing data. Paterson *et al.* (1985) have developed a demonstrator system, ESCORT, which analyses plant data to identify potential control and instrumentation failures, and provides operators with advice on crisis handling and avoidance.

To keep the technology within the realms of human understanding and control, Michie (e.g. 1982) argues for a *human window* into an expert system's operations. The human window is determined by the human brain's own limitations on memory and calculation, which Michie (1982) defines as 10^{10} bits and 20 binary discriminations respectively. Put another way, the notion of a human window depends on a system being both "executable" by, and "intelligible" to, a system user. Intelligibility is said to increase as the number of patterns to be processed decreases, while executability is inversely related to the amount of search required. On this basis, exhaustive minimax search procedures are intelligible but not (humanly) executable, and table-lookup procedures are executable but not intelligible. In order to preserve intelligibility, Michie (1982) proposes a structured approach to machine induction, one which restricts rule complexity. Each rule would be allowed a maximum of seven subpatterns — in accordance with Miller's (1956) estimate of human short-term memory capacity.

The understandability of rules in expert systems has received a lot of attention. Some of the main findings and recommendations in this area (see e.g. Welbank, 1983) include:

- *rule size* In the medical field, a typical rule may have three conditons and one action (Welbank, 1983, p.40). Following Michie (see above), seven conditions would seem to be a desirable maximum. Rules can be made smaller by introducing intermediate concepts.
- *grain size* Granularity refers to the level of detail at which a system represents its concepts. Whether this is "coarse" or "fine", it should correspond to the level employed by the system user.
- *complexity* Disjunctive conditions ("or"), negation ("not"), quantifiers ("some", "all", etc.) and nested conditions are all well known in cognitive psychology as causing understanding difficulties (e.g. Johnson-Laird and Wason, 1977), and should be used minimally, or not at all.

How uncertainty is expressed within a rule formalism also has implications for intelligibility. However, because the representation of uncertainty is a major research theme in its own right , this research is dealt with separately in a later section (5.6.6).

5.6.5   The explicit representation of knowledge

Conventional computer systems can be viewed as comprising two main components: "program" and "data". The program is typically an algorithmic procedure, perhaps written in a language like COBOL or PASCAL. Data refers to the information manipulated by the program — held in database files, working storage, etc. This organization fails to make explicit the relationships inherent in the data, or the control knowledge which is contextually-embedded in the program code. Such systems, particularly when they are very large, prove difficult to develop, maintain or understand.

By constrast, a characteristic feature of expert systems, from DENDRAL and MYCIN onwards, has been the attempt to improve intelligibility through a knowledge-based approach. An expert system's knowledge base encodes information in a way designed to capture its meaning — that is, as modular chunks of knowledge (facts, rules, etc.), which make explicit the relationships among items of data and other entities within some domain. Furthermore, much of the control knowledge embedded in an algorithmic procedure, can be represented declaratively as say, rules, within an expert system. This means that in comparison with previous types of information process-ing system, expert systems typically have a larger declarative compo-nent (the knowledge base) and a smaller procedural component (the inference engine). [For further discussion of the relative merits of procedural and declarative formalisms see Winograd (1975) or Barr and Feigenbaum (1981].

Despite the gains in system intelligibility the use of declarative formalisms has brought, it has become apparent that a great deal of knowledge remains effectively "compiled" into conventional rule-based expert systems (e.g. Aikins, 1983; Clancey, 1983). For exam-ple, Clancey (1983) found that the following types of knowledge were not explicitly represented in MYCIN:

● the *strategic* knowledge underlying the ordering of rules, and the ordering of rule conditions (these jointly exert a major influence on system behaviour given MYCIN's backward-chaining infer-encing mechanism)
● the *structural* knowledge implicit in the hierarchical organization of the MYCIN rule base
● the *support* knowledge which provides the justification for the inclusion of individual rules in the knowledge base

Clancey (1983) suggests that the implicit nature of such know-ledge helps explain why MYCIN proved difficult to modify by other than the original rule authors. It also prevented Clancey from directly adapting MYCIN to support a tutoring role. A complete reorganiza-tion of the MYCIN knowledge base was required for this purpose, implemented in the NEOMYCIN system (Clancey and Letsinger, 1981). Here intelligibility is enhanced by representing strategies explicitly as meta-rules (i.e. as rules that control the invocation of other rules). An alternative approach is adopted in CENTAUR (Aikins, 1983). In this system a hybrid knowledge representation — frames and production rules — is used to make explicit the context in which individual rules are routinely invoked. Small sets of rules are stored in the slots of different hypothesis frames, and are only considered for "firing" when the parent frame is itself activated.

Keravnou and Johnson (1986) have taken the explication of strategic knowledge a step further. In their "competent expert systems" methodology each diagnostic strategy (or sub-strategy) is represented as a task frame, which makes explicit the dynamic context in which a particular strategy is invoked. So, different frame slots specify different aspects: the conditions that "enable" a strategy to be invoked; those that "disable" it or which allow a disabling condition to be "relaxed"; the sub-tasks that must be achieved if the strategy is to succeed, and so on.

How much futher expert system researchers can take the process of knowledge explication is not yet clear. At present, the tendency is to see every move in the direction of greater explicitness as necessarily beneficial. However, a highly explicit representation of domain knowledge is at odds with what is known about the compiled nature of much expert knowledge. There is also a danger that explicit representations will result in distorted models of expert reasoning, since inferencing methods are closely linked to particular representation formalisms.

5.6.6 The qualitative treatment of uncertainty

A great deal has been written about the representation of uncertainty in expert systems. Conventional decision support systems have used techniques based on probability theory, such as Bayes' Theorem, to handle uncertainty in a rigorous, quantifiable fashion. In knowledge-based expert systems various *ad hoc* combinations of logic and probability theory have been employed. MYCIN (Shortliffe, 1976) and PROSPECTOR (Duda, Gaschnig and Hart, 1979) are two well-known systems using such ad hoc quantitative methods. MYCIN is illustrative of the kind of techniques currently in use. Rules in the knowledge base have "certainty factors" attached to them. A certainty factor is a number in the range -1.0 to 1.0 expressing the strength of belief that the conclusion of the rule is true, assuming all its premises are true. During a consultation these values combine to yield an overall confidence estimate attached to the system's advice.

Our concern here is not with the shortcomings of existing techniques from a theoretical or technical standpoint — although these are by no means trivial (e.g. Rich, 1983; White, 1984). Rather, it is with the lack of correlation between such techniques and how uncertainty is normally processed in human cognition. Earlier (Section 2.4.2) we reviewed psychological research indicating that people are more skilled and feel more comfortable handling uncertainty in a qualitative rather than a quantitative fashion. [This is not to identify qualitative approaches exclusively with human cognition, or quantitative methods with formal AI. For instance, many models of human pattern recognition are amenable to rigorous statistical expression and testing (Reed, 1972); and, equally, a formalized, qualitative treatment of uncertainty in AI is also possible (e.g. Cohen, 1985, see below).]. A number of qualitative techniques are now available for improving the psychological validity and/or intelligibility of how expert systems handle uncertainty:

(1) Fox, Barber and Bardhan (1980) found that a forward-chaining production rule system, PSYCO, in which medical diagnostic knowledge was expressed entirely non-numerically as production rules, performed as well as a Bayesian statistical system fed with comparable data. Each production rule simply encoded the empirical link between a small set of clinical data (condition part) and a particular disease (action part). Fox (1982) suggests that this categorical form is more like experts' own representations of facts than are purely quantitative estimates of likelihood. At the same time it is a more intelligible form, making it easier for the user to test and trace the system's reasoning on other cases (Fox, 1982).

(2) Human judgment under uncertainty appears governed in part by *availability* (see Section 2.4.2). This theory states that the more available a bit of stored information is, the more readily it comes to mind, and the more impact it will have on subsequent decision making. Fox (1980) captured this idea in an experimental production system simulating aspects of clinical decision–making. The bulk of rules in the rule base expressed learnt symptom–disease links, with the relative strength of particular disease-symptom pairs reflected in the ordering of the rule conditions. The interpreter was sensitive to this ordering, so that the more "certain" hypotheses got triggered and tested first. Again, this simulation compared favourably with a Bayesian system in an experimental trial.

(3) Along with availability, *representativeness* is the other main "heuristic" identified by Kahneman and Tversky (Kahneman, Slovic and Tversky, 1982; see Section 2.4.2) as exerting a major influence on human decision-making under conditions of uncertainty. This has been explicitly formalized into a qualitative technique for handling uncertainty in expert systems. The paper by Cohen *et al.* (1985) should be consulted for further details. More generally, any system in which test cases are judged on

their computed similarity (or degree of match) to hypothesis "prototypes" is operating in accordance with the representativeness principle. PIP (Pauker *et al.*, 1976) is one example discussed earlier in the chapter (Section 5.3.2).

(4) Most recently, Fox (1984a) has sketched another qualitative approach to uncertainty, based in part on his intuitions as an English speaker. He suggests that the 50 to 100 words in English for describing facts and data ("possible", "probable", etc.) can be arranged into a hierarchy of belief terms. These can then be used to represent people's beliefs "qualitatively with an explicit semantics, not numerically with an implicit semantics" (Fox, 1984a, p. 22). He observes that for such a scheme to become generally accepted, agreement about the relative precedence of belief terms would first be needed. In the meantime, designers could be left to define these relations explicitly — but arbitrarily — in rules, as the domain requires. The following rule from Fox (1984a) illustrates the approach:

> IF   Patient *could be* suffering from disease
> AND   Disease is *definitely* fatal
> THEN   Patient *may be* in danger

(5) Earlier (Section 5.6.5) it was noted how Clancey (1983) and others have sought to explicate the knowledge compiled into uniform knowledge bases consisting largely of empirical rules. Cohen and Greenberg (1983) make a similar point in relation to uncertainty. They argue that numerical estimates of uncertainty are just a summary of the reasons people have for believing/disbelieving a particular hypothesis, which become inaccessible when represented numerically. On this view if an intelligent reasoner is normally able to discriminate among these reasons then the summary representation is inadequate (Cohen, 1985). This is true, for example, where two statements are adjudged equally "probable", but only one can be proven. Cohen (1985) presents an AI approach to reasoning about uncertainty based on such qualitative considerations. The implication of this type of approach for knowledge acquisition is that experts should be required to justify their expressions of uncertainty. But this is likely to prove difficult in view of the inaccessible and highly compiled nature of much expert thinking (see Chapter 2).

(6) A combination of qualitative and quantitative methods has also been advocated. In the context of medical expert systems, Szolovits and Pauker (1978) propose a heuristic process of

hypothesis formation, followed by the weighing of evidence for and against each hypothesis. In short: "categorical proposes, probabilistic disposes". Similarly, Spiegelhalter and Knill-Jones (1984) conclude that a synthesis between statistical and knowledge-based techniques could overcome many of the long-standing criticisms of statistical decision-support systems. It should be apparent, though, that cognitive emulation is not the primary concern of these researchers.

5.7 EMULATING NEURAL PROCESSING

5.7.1 Introduction

So far we have tacitly assumed that if a cognitive model can be implemented in an expert system, then traditional AI will provide the necessary techniques. [Traditional AI seeks to represent knowledge of the world in formal symbols, enabling programs to be written which instruct a computer how to make inferences by manipulating these symbols.] In this section we briefly consider a radically different AI paradigm — one inspired by current neurological models of how the brain works. This approach to cognitive emulation has yet to be applied in expert systems work (to the author's knowledge), but is outlined here because of its potential future importance.

5.7.2 Rationale

AI has been an active area of research since the 1950s. The relative lack of progress in the intervening period has led to some disillusionment with the dominant AI paradigm based on symbol manipulation. One doubt is whether serial processing programs — however fast — can ever approach the power of human thinking. Another concerns the inpracticality of writing all the detailed instructions needed for a program to respond intelligently to unexpected events.

The slow progress of symbolic AI has provided the impetus for an alternative "connectionist" approach, which is modelled closely on the computational properties of the human brain. These properties include (Feldman, 1985; Hinton, 1985):

- a neural impulse takes a few milliseconds to be generated (about a million times slower than the basic computing speed of modern computers)
- a human can perform a simple task such as picture naming in around 500 milliseconds, or about 100 steps (the best available AI programs require millions of time steps to perform comparable tasks)
- the cortex of the human brain contains some 100 billion neurons

● each neuron is connected with up to about 10 000 others
● the human brain is a massively parallel natural computer

The connectionists argue that our knowledge is stored in the strength of inter-neuronal connections, and that thinking somehow emerges from the process of these connections forming and reforming. Massively parallel computational models of vision, natural language, knowledge representation, learning, etc. are currently under construction (see, for example, the papers in Rumelhart *et al.*, 1986).

5.7.3 Distinguishing features
The main features that distinguish the connectionist approach from traditional AI are (*Economist*, 1985):

(1) A belief that hardware matters — that symbolic processing cannot be abstracted from the hardware in which it is carried out.
(2) Connectionist models imply massively parallel computer architectures (although they can be simulated on serial digital computers).
(3) In connectionist machines memory and processing are diffusely distributed throughout the network, with little central control.
(4) Connectionist models are largely unprogrammed: only general instructions are given. The system reaches a solution by ungovernedly trying out different connections in the network until it settles into a stable state, i.e. no detailed algorithms or rules are involved.

Fig. 5.5 illustrates in highly simplified form some typical features of connectionist networks. Elements (e.g. neurons, processing units) are linked by connections of differing strengths, represented here by an integer. The plus and minus signs denote a positive or negative link respectively. A double-headed arrow indicates a symmetrical connection rather than an asymmetrical one (single-headed). The diagram also hints at the essentially probabilistic nature of problem solving activity in many connectionist models.

5.7.4 Assessment
The connectionist approach has not gone unchallenged. Theoretical critisms include:

● It has not yet been adequately explained how high-level symbolic manipulation (e.g. perception) can arise from low-level energy states (e.g. pattern recognition).

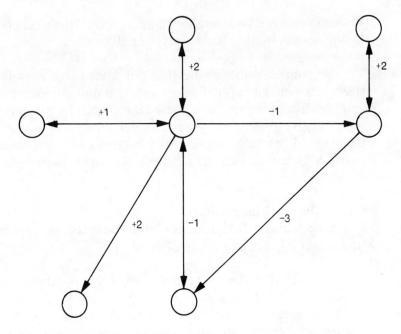

Fig. 5.5 — An illustrative connectionist network.

● To build a connectionist network able to simulate human thinking
  would require a machine with more connections than currently
  seems possible.
● Connectionist models do not offer an alternative to symbolic AI,
  because the difference is essentially one of level. That is, connectionist networks *may* represent how symbolic processing is implemented in the human brain — but symbolic processing is not
  dependent on this (or any other) "implementation language".
● The development of a connectionist network may depend heavily
  on careful prior structuring by the theorist, rather than developing
  purely in accordance with general principles (Anderson, 1983a).

More immediately, the special hardware required to make massively parallel connectionist models a practical option for knowledge
engineering is still being developed, while many theoretical issues in
connectionist modelling remain to be resolved (Feldman, 1985;
Hinton, 1985). There is a more fundamental objection, however.
That is to say, the human engineering objectives of expert systems —
explicit knowledge representation, intelligible reasoning, explanation, etc. — are inconsistent with the nature of connectionist models.
As already noted, knowledge is embedded in the strength of connections: the reasoning process is diffuse, probabilistic and highly

parallel — in short, system operation is unintelligible to a normal adult. Nevertheless, if it becomes apparent that some types of intelligent problem solving can only be simulated using a connectionist framework, then expert system designers will need to resolve the human engineering problem that is posed. This issue is explored further in Section 5.8.

5.8 GENERAL DISCUSSION

A large amount of work in expert systems and related fields is relevant to the subject of cognitive emulation. Even restricting the scope of this chapter to such central expert system topics as knowledge elicitation and representation, problem solving and system architecture, has left a lot of ground to cover. This chapter has aimed to provide a representative survey of important work in this area. Six broad approaches to cognitive emulation have been distinguished based principally on the level at which the emulation of human cognition is addressed (see Fig. 5.1). In each case I have tried to describe and evaluate the major development work, as well as identify some of the outstanding research issues.

Having considered each approach individually, it remains to consider the different approaches in combination. This is an important and unavoidable issue for two reasons. First, it may be difficult to emulate human cognition at one level without giving thought to emulation issues at proximate levels. Second, different approaches can confer different knowledge engineering benefits — offering a big incentive for a combined design solution. In simplified form, the main benefits offered by the six outlined approaches to emulation are:

(1) *Individual expert* Emulation facilitates the effective elicitation, representation and utilization of an individual expert's knowledge for system construction.
(2) *Domain expertise* Accurate formalization of domain knowledge, explication of typical reasoning strategies, etc.
(3) *Expert cognition* Fast, accurate and "non-brittle" expert-level performance.
(4) *User cognition* Ensuring usability by modelling the knowledge, expectations and preferences of the intended user group.
(5) *Human information processing* Matching system characteristics to human cognition for intelligibility. To perform difficult "human" tasks.
(6) *Neural processing models* Still at an early research stage, but ultimately for solving complex synthetic problems.

There are thus clear benefits to be achieved from a strategy of emulation encompassing a variety of approaches. Unfortunately, the design implications of different approaches are often contradictory — a point illustrated by Table 5.5, which contrasts the design features best suited to achieving expert-level performance and user intelligibility respectively. The performance-oriented features are characteristic of approaches which emulate expert problem solving [(1), (2) or (3)], or which reflect more general models of human problem solving [(5) and (6)]; whereas the features facilitating intelligibility are associated more with emulating specific user groups (4), and adaptations to the limitations of human information processing (5).

Table 5.5 — Design features facilitating expert-level performance and intelligibility

Expert system attribute	Performance	Intelligibility
System Architecture	Non-modular (e.g. distributed processing and memory)	Modular
Processing Mode	Parallel	Serial
Reasoning Strategies	Expert-oriented	User-oriented
Problem Formulation	Expert-oriented	User-oriented
Domain Conceptualization	Expert-oriented	User-oriented
Representation Language	Low level	High level
Knowledge	Compiled Procedural	Explicit Declarative
Knowledge Chunks	Relatively large and complex	Relatively small and simple

The question then arises : how can approaches to cognitive emulation with such conflicting design implications be combined? The basis for an architectural solution was mentioned in relation to user emulation (Section 5.5). In this solution — exemplified by the system architecture of intelligent front ends (Bundy, 1984), the Interviewer/Reasoner model (Gerring, Shortliffe and van Melle, 1982), UMFE (Sleeman, 1984), etc. — two main system elements are distinguished. As shown in Fig. 5.6, the user interacts only with a front-end sub-system modelled on the intended user group and optimised for intelligibility. This module would also communicate with a back-end performance program modelled on expert cognition or any other useful model of human problem solving (e.g. a connectionist model).

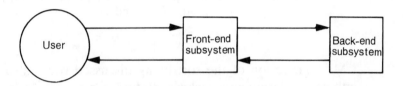

Fig. 5.6 — An outline system architecture for combining user-intelligibility (front end) and expert-level performance (back end).

There are many research issues outstanding with this type of architecture — not least the development of AI techniques for translating between the two modules (see Bundy, 1984). But modularization along these lines may offer the only viable solution for combining emulation approaches which fundamentally conflict in their design implications.

In Section 4.1.4 we noted the related problem of emulating the (distinctive) knowledge organization and reasoning strategies of several experts within a single system. A modular solution may also be considered here. One possibility is described by Lambird, Lavine and Kanal (1984): for certain purposes expert system can be organized as a co-operating community of experts, with each "specialist" comprising its own knowledge base and corresponding inference mechanism. Lambird et al. (1984) are primarily concerned with such distributed problem solving expert systems for use in applications with very large information and processing loads; for example, image understanding. Equally, however, it might provide a technique to enable the cognitive emulation of a number of experts within an integrated system. Fig. 5.7 illustrates this possibility as an elaboration of Fig. 5.6.

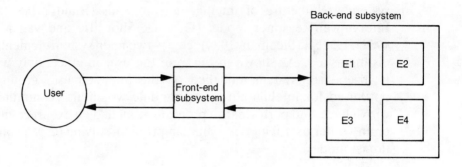

Fig. 5.7 — At outline system architecture for integrating the cognitive models of four experts (E1–4) and the intended user group (front end).

Modularization of the sort being discussed could also serve to combine emulation approaches with formal methods. Indeed, this is essentially what intelligent front ends (Bundy, 1984) are already doing. The "front end" is a friendly interface modelled on the user's understanding of a domain and preferred mode of interaction, while the "back end" is a complex statistical package, a relational database system, etc.

The potential for substantial design conflicts *within* the emulation strategy has gone largely unremarked in earlier discussions of the subject (e.g. Fox, 1982; Slatter, 1985). One reason is that under favourable conditions the different levels of approach to emulation can probably be fluently combined. Consider, for example, the following conditions:

● the task is of a relatively simple, analytic kind such as classification
● domain knowledge is largely empirical in nature, expressable as IF–THEN rules
● the amount of domain knowledge is relatively small
● the system users are themselves experts or partial experts

Under such conditions expert knowledge can be expressed in a declarative intelligible form without too much distortion; there is no significant conflict in conceptualization, reasoning strategies, etc. between experts and system users; and the cognitive models suitable for modelling the task — i.e. "pure" production systems — can be tailored to give intelligble behaviour. These conditions are approximated in the case of PSYCO (Fox et al., 1980), a clinical diagnostic system which manages to combine the emulation of established cognitive principles, intelligible knowledge representation and reasoning, and fidelity to expert cognition within an adapted production rule system.   However, the emulation approach can be expected to become increasingly fragmented as one moves away from these favourable conditions towards situations involving:

- complex synthetic tasks such as design
- more varied types of knowledge (e.g. temporal, spatial, causal)
- very large amounts of knowledge
- system users who are complete domain novices

It is under conditions such as these that the use of modular system architectures becomes a relevant design option.

There are thus grounds for supposing that different approaches to emulation can, in principle at least, be combined — though in different ways according to circumstances. It is also necessary to consider whether any conditions exist in which a single one of the six described approaches would be sufficient for a given knowledge engineering purpose. A possible scenario is where a piece of expert software is required to fulfill a highly specialised, but essentially limited task. For example, an autonomous expert system module embedded in a real-time process control application might have little need for a user interface, allowing optimization on expert cognition. The role the expert system is designed to perform for the user is clearly important in this regard. Arguably, pure problem solving systems require less elaborate user interfaces than systems engaging in co-operative problem solving with the user (see Section 5.4). Even so, the requirement of the system designer for modularity, intelligibility, etc. suggests that usability will almost always be a consideration.

The flowchart in Fig. 5.8 is an attempt to formalize in summary form the guidlines for selecting and combining emulation approaches given above. It can be seen as a companion to the earlier decision rule (Fig. 4.1). The difference is this: Fig. 4.1 is intended to help identify *when* a strategy of cognitive emulation is worth pursuing; while Fig 5.8 aims to assist in identifying *which* particular emulation approach(es) to pursue. The flowchart reflects the fact that formal methods alone will sometimes be sufficient to generate a design solution. It also allows for a combination of formal methods with emulation approaches. Failure to find a workable singular or combined solution leads to either abandonment of the proposed system or a respecification of requirements.

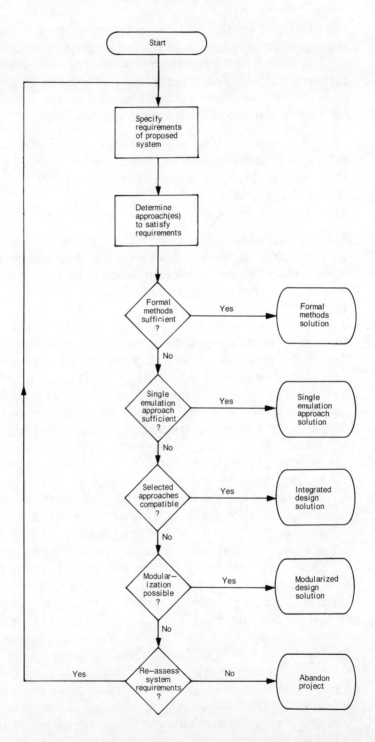

Fig. 5.8 — Flowchart for selecting/combining emulation approaches.

5.9 SUGGESTED READING

At present no general textbooks covering this subject area in greater depth are available. The reader is thus advised to follow up references given in this chapter which coincide with their specific interests.

6

Conclusion

This book has provided an assessment of the cognitive emulation strategy in expert system design. In this final chapter the main conclusions of previous chapters are reviewed. A more designer-oriented summary is also provided, for the benefit of knowledge engineers interested in adopting an emulation approach.

6.1 SUMMARY OF MAIN CONCLUSIONS

6.1.1 The principle of cognitive emulation

Chapter 1 introduced the term cognitive emulation, which denotes an approach to expert system design in which human thinking is the guiding principle. Domain experts are one obvious focus for attempts at emulation; system users another. An emulation approach implies a close coupling between knowledge engineering and cognitive psychology. The psychological models, methods and techniques of the cognitive scientist provide a rationale for the emulation strategy. Cognitive emulation is distinguished from cognitive modelling *per se* by its engineering perspective. At present the number of research projects in which cognitive emulation is an explicit concern is growing, but outside of research centres awareness of the emulation principle remains limited.

6.1.2 Human expert thinking

Chapter 2 reviewed our present understanding of human expert thinking. Cognitive research in this area confirms the belief that human expertise is essentially a knoweldge-based skill, acquired through many years of practice in a specialist domain. Prodigious amounts of knowledge are acquired, and this goes a long way in explaining the superior performance of domain experts compared to novices. However, qualitative changes in knowledge organization and reasoning strategies also play an important role. They enable the expert to rely less on formal problem solving methods, and more on pattern recognition and memory. Expert cognition is better adapted than novice cognition to the unique characteristics of a particular domain.

Frequently observed correlates of developing expertise include enhanced working memory capacity, speed-up and tuning of decision processes, and proceduralization of task-related knowledge. Such changes can be classed as "benefits", since they tend to improve task performance. However, the development of expertise also has its associated costs. In particular, proceduralized knowledge and auto-mated processes are relatively inaccessible, making it harder for experts to report accurately on their thinking. So, in a sense, expert-level performance is achieved at the expense of intelligibility.

6.1.3 Arguments

Chapter 3 assembled the principal arguments for and against cogni-tive emulation. The main conclusion reached was as follows. Cogni-tive emulation is a strategy for expert system design that can be neither explicitly rejected nor unselectively pursued. On the one hand, a significant element of cognitive modelling seems inherent in knowledge engineering, and is desirable in order to promote expert-level performance, user acceptance, effective knowledge acquisition, and a principled approach to design. Militating against a pure, unselective strategy, on the other hand, are the known weaknesses, limitations and inefficiencies of human thinking, the desire to improve on expert-level performance, and the requirement that an expert system should embody the specialist skill of several experts.

6.1.4 Constraining and facilitating factors

Chapter 4 examined the viability of cognitive emulation at a more practical level; considering which are the factors likely to constrain and facilitate a cognitive approach. Some of these factors cut both ways:

● The areas in which an emulation approach might come into conflict with established knowledge engineering objectives such as efficiency, modifiability and accuracy were carefully detailed. In other areas, though, cognitive emulation was shown to coincide rather than conflict with existing knowledge engineering objectives.

● The relative immaturity of both cognitive science and expert systems technology represent constraints on applying an emulation strategy at present. However, developments in these fields are likely to facilitate a cognitive approach in the future.

The inherent emulability (or not) of human cognition in artificial systems is another possible constraint on emulation. However, in practice, the effects of this factor are difficult to disentangle from the constraining effects of present day technology and scientific understanding. Two clear benefits of cognitive emulation emerged. First, despite its limitations, cognitive psychology can serve as a useful source of ideas and techniques for expert system builders. Second, the utility of an emulation approach tends to increase with task difficulty — especially for very large, highly complex and "synthetic" tasks that are unamenable to formal methods. A decision to adopt a strategy of emulation needs to consider the constraints and facilitating factors operating in a particular case. Fig. 4.1 is designed to help with such a decision.

6.1.5 Applications and different approaches
Chapter 5 reviewed existing and potential applications of cognitive emulation in expert system design. As currently applied by expert system researchers, cognitive emulation is far from being a unitary strategy. On the contrary, a survey of the published literature reveals a multiplicity of approaches, inspired by different cognitive models, knowledge engineering objectives, etc. Six basic approaches were identified. These centred on modelling the cognitive processes representative of:

● an individual domain expert
● experts in a particular domain (e.g. clinical diagnosticians)
● human experts in general
● users
● people in general — human information processing perspective
● people in general — neural networks perspective

Several important points emerged from an assessment of these six approaches:

(1) Much of the valuable detail of human thinking can be captured and embodied in an expert system if appropriate tools and techniques are employed.
(2) Earlier research focused on emulating the individual expert's ability to solve a problem. However, this ignores the fact that in the real word experts perform a much wider range of cognitive functions, including tutoring, guidance and remedy negotiation.

Some recent research efforts have attempted to emulate the ability to engage in co-operative problem solving of this sort.

(3) A variety of techniques is also under development for emulating the knowledge organization and reasoning strategies characteristic of some specialistic domain, dynamic aspects of expert cognition, and relevant aspects of user cognition.

(4) The three-part system architecture of standard expert systems parallels the outline "architecture" for human cognition proposed by cognitive psychologists. This similarity is somewhat deceptive, however, as there are also significant differences between the two.

(5) For certain kinds of expert problem solving, it may prove necessary to model human thinking at a non-symbolic level — that is, in "massively parallel networks" modelled on human neural processing.

The issues raised by combining alternative approaches to emulation were considered, since each approach confers different knowledge engineering benefits. Under favourable conditions, different approaches can be integrated within a single system. On the other hand, where the approaches to be combined have contradictory design implications, a modularized design solution is recommended. Some general guidelines for selecting and combining emulation approaches were given.

6.2 SUMMARY OF DESIGN ADVICE

Implicitly and explicitly, earlier chapters of this book contain many pieces of advice about designing expert systems from a cognitive perspective. For the benefit of expert system practioners interested in adopting a cognitive approach this advice is summarized below. The advice given should be read as a provisional set of suggestions, rather than as precise methodological guidelines.

(1) *Deciding whether to adopt an emulation strategy (see also Section 4.3)*
Only adopt an explicit strategy of cognitive emulation if the answer to all the following questions is yes.

● Is it impossible to satisfy all the requirements of a proposed expert system application using formal methods?
● Can a cognitive model be found corresponding to the requirements of the proposed application?
● Can the cognitive model be implemented as a computer program?

● Is the cognitive model powerful/predictive enough to support the proposed application?

(2) *Selecting a particular emulation strategy (see also Section 5.8)*

if   All the requirements of a proposed application can be satisfied using a single emulation approach

then   Adopt that emulation approach

if   The requirements of a proposed application can only be satisfied by a combination of emulation approaches

and   The approaches have compatible design implications

then   Adopt an integrated system design solution

if   The requirements of a proposed application can only be satisfied by a combination of emulation approaches

and   The approaches have incompitible design implications

then   Adopt a modularized system design solution

(3) *Knowledge elicitation (see also Section 5.2)*

● Match the elicitation technique to the type of knowledge to be elicited.

● Use a variety of elicitation techniques (expert knowledge is rarely of just one type).

● Give consideration to techniques widely used in cognitive psychology such as protocol analysis, Repertory Grid Technique, conceptual sorting and memory probing.

● Be alert to rejection or distortion of elicited knowledge due to the constraints imposed by inappropriate expert system tools (knowledge representations, inference engines, etc.).

● Knowledge analysis, and the use of intermediate representations for coding elicited knowledge, are two techniques for overcoming such distorting influences.

● Be alert to the potential sources of invalidity in verbal data.

(4) *Knowledge representation (see especially Section 5.6)*

● Match the knowledge representation to the type of knowledge to be represented.

● Use a variety of knowledge representations (expert knowledge is rarely of just one type).

● For user intelligibility, represent human knowledge explicitly.

● For expert-level problem solving, represent human knowledge in a compiled, proceduralized form.

● For both, consider a modularized system design — with know-

ledge represented in a user-oriented and in an expert-oriented form.
- The size, complexity and grain size of knowledge units (e.g. production rules) should accord with human cognition.
- Production rules are a natural representation for certain kinds of human pattern-directed knowledge.
- The interconnectivity of human long-term memory is appropriately modelled in an associative network.
- Spatial and temporal knowledge should be represented analogically.
- Cognitive prototypes can be represented as frames, with the slots set to default (typical) values.

(5) *Knowledge utilization*
- Model the problem solving approach of an expert system on an appropriate domain expert.
- Represent expert reasoning strategies explicitly as meta-rules, task frames, etc.
- The prominence of pattern recognition in expert problem solving implies that forward inferencing should be a feature of *any* expert system modelled on human expertise.
- Breadth-first retrieval strategies (through a network) are a better approximation of human memory retrieval than either depth-first or serial searches through a set of independent knowledge elements.
- In general, human reasoning involves a subtle interplay of forward and backward inferencing, serial and parallel processes. Modelling this interplay should be an important objective for "cognitive emulators".
- The powerful pattern representation and pattern matching facilities offered by AI languages such as PROLOG can be exploited in emulating human pattern processing.
- Avoid Bayes' Rule, or any other formal method of approximate reasoning — unless there is evidence that the human expert is explicitly using such an approach. Consider the qualitative approaches listed in Section 5.6.6.
- An autonomous problem solving system is not always the most appropriate design solution. Try to identify and model the cognitive functions (e.g. critiquing, tutoring) that human experts are actually performing for users in a given application area.
- The cognitive function(s) the system is to perform should be identified at an early stage, so that knowledge acquisition can focus on relevant aspects of expert/user cognition.

(6) *Using the design advice*

There are two main ways in which the above advice might be used. Taken collectively, the suggestions represent elements of a *principled* approach to cognitive emulation in expert system design. Alternatively, individual bits of advice can be acted on in an *ad hoc* fashion, as opportunities or needs arise in a particular project. For most practical purposes, an *ad hoc* approach will remain the realistic option for some time to come. It accords with current knowledge engineering practice — which is eclectic and pragmatic — and with the current limitations of expert systems technology and cognitive psychology. As these constraints drop away, however, the scope for a principled approach will increase.

Glossary

algorithm   A detailed step-by-step procedure for performing a task that is guaranteed to succeed.

analogical representations   This is a class of knowledge representation formalisms in which there is a structural similarity between the representation and the situation that is represented. Examples include maps, models and diagrams. Analogical representations contrast with "propositional" representations, such as semantic networks and logic, which do not require this structural correspondence.

backward chaining   An inferencing strategy which involves working back from a conclusion or goal to see if the conditions that would make it true are satisfied. The strategy is appropriate in problem domains where the conclusions can be specified in advance; for example, electronic fault diagnosis.

declarative representations   In a declarative representation knowledge typically comprises a static collection of facts accompanied by a small set of procedures for manipulating them.

epistemology   The theory of the method or grounds for knowledge. In knowledge engineering, epistemological analysis is carried out to identify the basic classes of elements (e.g. "solutions"), relations (e.g. taxonomic), etc. underlying the verbal statements elicited from domain experts. Epistemological analysis offers a means of conceptualizing knowledge at a level distinct from the available representational technology.

forward chaining

An inferencing strategy which builds up from the available data about a problem to deduce conclusions. It is appropriate where the possible conclusions cannot be pre-specified, or where the number of conclusions is large relative to the number of initial problem states. For example, designing a computer hardware configuration.

frames

A common knowledge representation formalism in expert systems. A frame is a data structure for representing stereotyped situations in terms of "slots" and "fillers". For example, the frame for "chair" might contain a "number-of-legs" slot which, in the case of a prototypical chair, would have a filler value of "4 legs". Various types of information are attached to a frame, including information about how to use the frame.

heuristic

A "rule of thumb" method or aid to solving a problem. Unlike an algorithm, a heuristic is not guaranteed to succeed, but is useful in the majority of cases.

logic

One of the first knowledge representation formalisms used in AI. It enables conclusions to be deduced from initial premises using purely syntactic rules of inference. Logic is also the basis of such AI languages as PROLOG (PROgramming in LOGic).

procedural representations

In a procedural representation knowledge is contextually-embedded in procedures, e.g. computer algorithms.

production rule

A production rule is an item of knowledge which takes the form — IF this *condition* is true, THEN this *action* is appropriate. For example:

> IF   (a) the sun is shining, and
>   (b) the day is Sunday
> THEN   consider going fishing

production system

A production system is a type of AI progam consisting of three main elements:

(1) a knowledge base, comprising a set of production rules;
(2) a "working memory" consisting of data relevant to the current problem;
(3) a control program, called an "interpreter" or "inference engine".

The control program selectively fires rules in (1) based on the current state of (2). This cycle repeats until the program terminates.

scripts
A script is a frame-like structure specifically designed for representing typical sequences or events.

semantic network
A knowledge formalism in which information is represented as a set of nodes and links. The nodes represent concepts, and the links stand for the relationships between the concepts. For example, the concepts "eagle" and "bird" could be linked by the relationship "is a kind of".

References

Adelson, B. (1984) When Novices Surpass Experts: The Difficulty of a Task May Increase with Expertise. *Journal of Experimental Psychology: Learning, Memory and Cognition*, *10*, 483–495.

Aikins, J. S. (1983) Prototypical Knowledge for Expert Systems. *Artificial Intelligence*, *20*, 163–210.

Anderson, J. R. (1976) *Language, Memory and Thought*. Hillsdale, NJ: Erlbaum.

Anderson, J. R. (1983a) *The Architecture of Cognition*. Cambridge, MA: Harvard University Press.

Anderson, J. R. (1983b) Acquisition of Proof Skills in Geometry. In J. G. Carbonell, R. Michalski and T. Mitchell (Eds.), *Machine Learning, An Artificial Intelligence Approach*. San Francisco: Tioga.

Anderson, J. R. (1984) Cognitive Psychology. *Artificial Intelligence*, *23*, 1–11.

Anderson, J. R. (1985) *Cognitive Psychology and its Implications*. New York: Freeman.

Anderson, J. R. and Bower, G. H. (1973) *Human Associative Memory*. Washington, D. C.: Winston.

Anderson, J. R., Farrell, R. and Sauers, R. (1984) Learning to Program in Lisp. *Cognitive Science*, *8*, 87–129.

Arkes, H. R. and Freedman, M. R. (1984) A Demonstration of the Cost and Benefits of Expertise in Recognition Memory. *Memory and Cognition*, *12*, 84–89.

Baddeley, A. D. (1976) *The Psychology of Memory*. New York: Harper and Row.

Baddeley, A. D. (1981) The Concept of Working Memory: A View of its Current State and Probable Future Development. *Cognition*, *10*, 17–23.

Barr, A. and E. A. Feigenbaum (Eds.) (1981) *The Handbook of Artificial Intelligence*, Volume 1. Los Altos, California: Kaufman.

Barr, A. and E. A. Feigenbaum (Eds.) (1982) *The Handbook of Artificial Intelligence*, Volume 2. Los Altos, California: Kaufman.

Barsalou, L. W. and Bower, G. H. (1984) Discrimination Nets as Psychological Models. *Cognitive Science, 8*, 1–26.

Bartlett, F. C. (1932) *Remembering: A Study in Experimental and Social Psychology*. Cambridge: Cambridge University Press.

Bennett, J. S. (1985) ROGET: A Knowledge–based System for Acquiring the Conceptual Structure of an Expert System. *Journal of Automated Reasoning, 1*, 49–74.

Berry, D. C. and Broadbent, D. E. (1984) On the Relationship between Task Performance and Associated Verbalizable Knowledge. *Quarterly Journal of Experimental Pyschology, 36A*, 209–231.

Bhaskar, R. and Simon, H. A. (1977) Problem Solving in Semantically Rich Domains: An Example from Engineering Thermodynamics. *Cognitive Science, 1*, 193–215.

Bishop, P. (1986) *Fifth Generation Computers: Concepts, Implementations and Uses*. Chichester: Ellis Horwood.

Boden, M. A. (1977) *Artificial Intelligence and Natural Man*. Brighton: Harvester.

Boden, M. A. (1985) Lecture given at *Expert Systems 85*, University of Warwick, England.

Boose, J.H. (1984) Personal Construct Theory and the Transfer of Expertise. In *Proceedings of AAAI–84*, 27–33.

Boyle, C. D. B. (1985) Acquisition of Control and Domain Knowledge by Watching in a Blackboard Environment. In M. Merry (Ed.), *Expert Systems 85*. Cambridge: Cambridge University Press.

Bramer, M. A. (1984) Expert Systems: The Vision and the Reality. In M. A. Bramer (Ed.), *Research and Development in Expert Systems*. Cambridge: Cambridge University Press.

Bratko, I., Lavrac, N. and Mozetic, I. (1985) Kardio-E: An Expert System for Electrocardiographic Analysis of Cardiac Arrhymthias. Paper given at *First International Expert Systems Conference*, London (October 1985).

Breuker, J. A. and Wielinga, R. J. (1983a) *Analysis Techniques for Knowledge Based Systems*, Part 1. Report 1.1, Esprit Project 12, University of Amsterdam.

Breuker, J. A. and Wielinga, R. J. (1983b) *Analysis Techniques for*

Knowledge Based Systems, Part 2. Report 1.2, Esprit Project 12, University of Amsterdam.

Breuker, J. A. and Wielinga, R. J. (1983c) *Initial Analysis for Knowledge Based Systems: An Example*. Report 1.3a, Esprit Project 12, University of Amsterdam.

Breuker, J. A. and Wielinga, R. J. (1984) *Techniques for Knowledge Elicitation and Analysis*. Report 1.5, Esprit Project 12, University of Amsterdam.

Brooks, R. A. (1983) Model-based Three-dimensional Interpretation of Two-dimensional Images. *IEEE Transactions on Pattern Analysis and Machine Intelligence*, PAMI-5, 140–150.

Brown, J. S. and Burton, R. R. (1978) Diagnostic Models for Procedural Bugs in Basic Mathematical Skills. *Cognitive Science*, 2, 155–192.

Buchanan, B. G. (1982) New Research on Expert Systems. In J. E. Hayes, D. Michie and Y-H. Pao (Eds.), *Machine Intelligence 10*. Chichester: Ellis Horwood.

Buchanan, B. G. and Feigenbaum E. A. (1978) DENDRAL and Meta-DENDRAL ; Their Application Dimension. *Artificial Intelligence*, 11, 5–24.

Bundy, A. (1984) Intelligent Front Ends. In M. A. Bramer (Ed.), *Research and Development in Expert Systems*. Cambridge: Cambridge University Press.

Card, S. K., Moran, T. P. and Newell, A. (1983) *The Psychology of Human-Computer Interaction*. Hillsdale, NJ: Erlbaum.

Cendrowska, J. and Bramer, M. A. (1984) A Rational Reconstruction of the MYCIN Consultation System. *International Journal of Man-Machine Studies*, 20, 229–317.

Chase, W. G. and Ericsson, K. A. (1982) Skill and Working Memory. In G. H. Bower (Ed.), *The Psychology of Learning and Motivation*, Vol 16. New York: Academic Press.

Chase, W. G. and Simon, H. A. (1973) Perception in Chess. *Cognitive Psychology*, 4, 55–81.

Chi, M. T. H., Feltovich, P. J. and Glaser, R. (1981) Categorizaton and Representation of Physics Problems by Experts and Novices. *Cognitive Science*, 5, 121–152.

Clancey, W. J. (1983) The Epistemology of a Rule-Based Expert System: A Framework for Explanation. *Artificial Intelligence*, 20, 215–251.

Clancey, W. J. (1984) Knowledge Acquisition for Classification Expert Systems. *Proceedings of the ACM'84 Annual Conference*, 11–14.

Clancey, W. J. (1985) Heuristic Classification. *Artificial Intelligence*, **27**, 215–251.

Clancey, W. J. and Letsinger, R. (1981) NEOMYCIN: Reconfiguring a Rule-Based Expert System for Application to Teaching. In *Proceedings of the Seventh IJCAI*, 829–836.

Cohen, P. R. (1985) Heuristic Reasoning about Uncertainty: An Artificial Intelligence Approach. *Research Notes in AI 2*. Pitman: London.

Cohen, P., Davis, A., Day, D., Greenberg, M., Kjeldsen, R., Lander, S. and Loiselle, C. (1985) Representativeness and Uncertainty in Classification Systems. *AI Magazine*, **6**(3), 136–149.

Cohen, P. and Greenberg, M. (1983) A Theory of Heuristic Reasoning About Uncertainty. *AI Magazine*, **4**(2), 17–24.

Collins, A. M. and Loftus, E. F. (1975) A Spreading-Activation Theory of Semantic Processing. *Psychological Review*, **82**, 407–428.

Collins, H. M., Green, R. H. and Draper, R. C. (1985) Where's the Expertise? Expert Systems as a Medium of Knowledge Transfer. In M. Merry (Ed.), *Expert Systems 85*. Cambridge: Cambridge University Press.

Coombs, M. J. (Ed.) (1984) *Developments in Expert Systems*. London: Academic Press.

Coombs, M. and Alty, J. (1984) Expert Systems: An Alternative Paradigm. In M. J. Coombs (Ed.), *Developments in Expert Systems*. London: Academic Press. (Also in *International Journal of Man–Machine Studies*, **20**, 21–43.)

Daneman, M. and Carpenter, P. A. (1980) Individual Differences in Working Memory and Reading. *Journal of Verbal Learning and Verbal Behaviour*, **19**, 450–466.

Davis, R. (1982) Expert Systems: Where Are We? And Where Do We Go From Here? *The AI Magazine*, **3**(2), 3–22.

Davis, R. (1984) Reasoning from First Principles in Electronic Trouble-shooting. In M. J. Coombs (Ed.), *Developments in Expert Systems*. London: Academic Press. (Also in *International Journal of Man–Machine Studies*, **19**, 403–423 (1983).)

Davis, R. and King. J. (1977) An Overview of Production Systems. In E. Elcock and D. Michie (Eds.), *Machine Intelligence*, Vol 8. Chichester: Ellis Horwood.

de Groot, A. D. (1965) *Thought and Choice in Chess*. The Hague: Mouton.

de Kleer, J. and Brown, J. S. (1983) Assumptions and Ambiguities in

Mechanistic Mental Models. In D. Gentner and A. S. Stevens (Eds.), *Mental Models*. Hillsdale, NJ: Erlbaum.

Duda, R. O., Gaschnig, J. G. and Hart, P. E. (1979) Model Design in the PROSPECTOR Consultant System for Mineral Exploration. In D. Michie (Ed.) *Expert Systems in the Micro-electronic Age*. Edinburgh: Edinburgh Press.

Duda, R. O. and Shortliffe, E. H. (1983) Expert Systems Research. Science, **220**, 261–268.

Economist (1985) Seeking the Mind in the Pathways of the Machine. *Economist Magazine*, June 29th, 1985, 83–88.

Eisenstadt, M. and Kareev, Y. (1975) Aspects of Human Problem Solving: The Use of Internal Representations. In D. A. Norman and D. E. Rumelhart (Eds.), *Explorations of Cognition*. San Francisco: Freeman.

Elio, R. (1986) Representation of Similar Well-Learned Cognitive Procedures. *Cognitive Science*, **10**, 41–73.

Elio, R. and Anderson, J. R. (1981) Effects of Category Generalizations and Instance Similarity on Schema Abstraction. *Journal of Experimental Psychology: Human Learning and Memory*, **7**, 397–417.

Elstein, A., Shulman, L. and Sprafka, S. (1978) *Medical Problem Solving — An Analysis of Clinical Reasoning*. Cambridge, MA: Harvard University Press.

Ericsson, K. and Simon, H. A. (1980) Verbal Reports as Data. *Psychological Review*, **87**, 215–251.

Feldman, J. A. (1985) Connections: Massive Parallelism in Natural and Artificial Intelligence. *Byte* (April), 277–284.

Feltovich, P. J., Johnson, P. E., Moller, J. H. and Swanson, D. B. (1984) LCS: The Role and Development of Medical Knowledge in Diagnostic Expertise. In W. J. Clancey and E. H. Shortliffe (Eds.), *Readings in Medical Artificial Intelligence: The First Decade*. Reading, MA: Addison-Wesley.

Forbus, K. D. and Gentner, D. (1986) Learning in Physical Domains: Toward a Theoretical Framework. In R. S. Michalski, J. G. Carbonell and T. M. Mitchell (Eds.), *Machine Learning: An Artificial Intelligence Approach*, Vol. 2. Los Altos, CA: Kaufman.

Fox, J. (1980) Making Decisions Under the Influence of Memory. *Psychological Review*, **87**, 190–211.

Fox, J. (1982) Expertise in Man and Machine. Paper given at the Colloquium on *Applications of Knowledge-based (or Expert) Systems*. Institute of Electrical Engineers, Savoy Place, London.

Fox, J. (1983) *Intelligent Knowledge Based Systems and Man-machine Interaction: Final Report.* Alvey IKBS Architecture Study.

Fox, J. (1984a) Inferences about Beliefs and Values. Paper given at *Alvey IKBS Inference Research Theme Workshop*, Imperial College, London.

Fox, J. (1984b) Formal and Knowledge Based Methods in Decision Technology. *Acta Psychologica, 56,* 303–331.

Fox, J., Barber, D. and Bardhan, K. D. (1980) Alternatives to Bayes? A Quantitative Comparison with Rule-Based Diagnosis. *Methods of Information in Medicine, 19,* 210–215.

Fox, J., Alvey, P. and Meyers, C. (1983) Decision Technology and Man–Machine Interaction: The PROPS Package. In J. Fox (Ed.), *Expert Systems 83*, Churchill College, Cambridge.

Gammack, J. G. and Young, R. M. (1984) Psychological Techniques for Eliciting Knowledge. In M. A. Bramer (Ed.), *Research and Development in Expert Systems.* Cambridge: Cambridge University Press.

Garner, W. R. (1976) Interaction of Stimulus Dimensions in Concept and Choice Processes. *Cognitive Psychology, 8,* 98–123.

Gaschnig, J., Klahr, P., Pople, H., Shortliffe, E. and Terry, A. (1983) Evaluation of Expert Systems: Issues and Case Studies, In F. Hayes-Roth, D. A. Waterman, and D. B. Lenat (Eds.), *Building Expert Systems*, Reading, MA: Addison-Wesley.

Gentner, D. and Collins, A. (1981) Studies of Inference from Lack of Knowledge. *Memory and Cognition, 19,* 434–443.

Gentner, D. and Stevens, A. S. (Eds.) (1983) *Mental Models.* Hillsdale, NJ: Erlbaum.

Gerring, P. F., Shortliffe, E. H. and van Melle, W. (1982) The Interviewer/Reasoner Model: An Approach to Improving System Responsiveness in Interactive AI Systems. *AI Magazine,* 3(4), 24-27.

Gick, M. L. and Holyoak, K. J. (1983) Schema Induction and AnalogicalTransfer. *Cognitive Psychology, 15,* 1–38.

HaKong, L. and Hickman, F. R. (1985) Expert Systems Techniques: An Application in Statistics. In M. Merry (Ed.), *Expert Systems 85.* Cambridge: Cambridge University Press.

Hammond, N. and Barnard, P. (1985) Dialogue Design: Characteristics of User Knowledge. In A. Monk (Ed.), *Fundamentals of Human-Computer Interaction.* London: Academic Press.

Hasling, D. W., Clancey, W. J. and Rennels, G. (1984) Strategic Explanations for a Diagnostic Consultation System. In M. J.

Coombs (Ed.), *Developments in Expert Systems*. London: Academic press. (Also in *International Journal of Man-Machine Studies*, **20**, 3–19.)

Hayes, P. J. (1984) On the Differences Between Psychology and AI. In M. Yazdani and A. Narayanan (Eds.), *Artificial Intelligence: Human Effects*. Chichester: Ellis Horwood.

Hayes-Roth, B. (1978) Implications of Human Pattern Processing for the Design of Artificial Knowledge Systems. In D. A. Waterman and F. Hayes-Roth (Eds.) *Pattern-Directed Inference Systems*. London: Academic Press.

Hayes-Roth, B. (1983) The Blackboard Architecture: A General Framework for Problem Solving? Heuristic Programming Project, Report No. HPP–83–30.

Hayes-Roth, B. and Hayes-Roth, F. (1979) A Cognitive Model of Planning. *Cognitive Science*, **3**, 275-310.

Hayes-Roth, F. (1984) The Knowledge-based Expert System: A Tutorial. *Computer* (September), 11–28.

Hayes-Roth, F. (1985) Knowledge-Based Expert Systems — The State of the Art in the US. *Knowledge Engineering Review*, **1**(2), 18–27.

Hayes-Roth, F., and Waterman, D. A. (1978) Principles of Pattern-Directed Inference Systems. In D. A. Waterman and F. Hayes-Roth (Eds.), *Pattern-Directed Inference Systems*. London: Academic Press.

Hayes-Roth, F., Waterman, D. A., and Lenat, D. B. (Eds.) (1983) *Building Expert Systems*. Reading, MA: Addison-Wesley.

Hinton, G. E. (1985) Learning in Parallel Networks. *Byte* (April), 265–273.

Hunt, E. B., Marin, J. and Stone, P. J. (1966) *Experiments in Induction*. New York: Academic Press.

Hunter, I. M. L. (1977) Mental Calculation. In P. N. Johnson-Laird and P. C. Wason (Eds.), *Thinking: Readings in Cognitive Science*. Cambridge: Cambridge University Press.

Jackson, P. (1986) *Introduction to Expert Systems*. Reading, MA: Addison-Wesley.

Jansweiger, W. H. N., Elshout, J. J. and Wielinga, B. J. (1986) The Expertise of Novice Problem Solvers. *Proceedings of ECAI'86*, Vol. 1, 576–585.

Jeffries, R., Turner, A., Polson, P., and Atwood, M. (1981) The Processes Involved in Designing Software. In J. R. Anderson (Ed.), *Cognitive Skills and their Acquisition*. Hillsdale, NJ: Erlbaum.

Johnson, P. E., Duran, A. S., Hassebrock, F., Moller, J., Prietula,

M., Feltovich, P. J., and Swanson, D. B. (1981) Expertise and Error in Diagnostic Reasoning. *Cognitive Science*, **5**, 235–283.

Johnson, T. (1984) The Commercial Application of Expert System Technology. *Knowledge Engineering Review*, *1*(1) 15–25.

Johnson-Laird, P. N. (1982) Thinking as a Skill. *Quarterly Journal of Experimental Psychology*, **34A**, 1–29.

Johnson-Laird, P. N. and Wason, P. C. (Eds.) (1977) *Thinking: Readings in Cognitive Science*. Cambridge: Cambridge University Press.

Kahneman, D., Slovic, P., and Tversky, A. (Eds.) (1982) *Judgment under Uncertainty: Heuristics and Biases*. Cambridge: Cambridge University Press.

Kassirer, J. and Gorry, G. (1978) Clinical Problem Solving: A Behavioural Analysis. *Annals of Internal Medicine*, **89**, 245–255.

Keravnou, E. T. and Johnson, L. (1986) *Competent Expert Systems: A Case Study in Fault Diagnosis*. London: Kogan Page.

Kidd, A. L. (1985a) Human Factors Problems in the Design and Use of Expert Systems. In A. Monk (Ed.), *Fundamentals of Human-Computer Interaction*. London: Academic Press.

Kidd, A. L. (1985b) *Knowledge Elicitation — A Pragmatic Approach*. Lecture given at BCS Expert System Group Meeting, London (November).

Kidd, A. L. (1985c) What do User's Ask? — Some Thoughts on Diagnostic Advice. In M. Merry (Ed.), *Expert Systems 85*. Cambridge: Cambridge University Press.

Kolodner, J. L. (1984) Towards an Understanding of the Role of Experience in the Evolution from Novice to Expert. In M. J. Coombs (Ed.), *Developments in Expert Systems*. London: Academic Press. (Also in *International Journal of Man–Machine Studies*, **19**, 497–518 (1983).)

Kosslyn, S. M. (1980) *Image and Mind*. Cambridge, MA: Harvard University Press.

Kuhn, T. S. (1970) *The Structure of Scientific Revolutions*. 2nd Edition. Chicargo: University of Chicargo Press.

Kuipers, B. and Kassirer, J. P. (1984) Causal Reasoning in Medicine: Analysis of a Protocol. *Cognitive Science*, **8**, 363–385.

Lambird, B. A., Lavine, D. and Kanal, L. N. (1984) Distributed Architecture and Parallel Non-Directional Search for Knowledge-based Cartographic Feature Extraction Systems. In M. J. Coombs (Ed.), *Developments in Expert Systems*. London: Academic Press. (Also in *International Journal of Man–Machine Studies*, **20**, 107–120.)

Langlotz, C. P. and Shortliffe, E. H. (1984) Adapting a Consultation

System to Critique User Plans. In M. J. Coombs (Ed.), *Developments in Expert Systems*. London: Academic Press. (Also in *International Journal of Man–Machine Studies*, **19**, 476–496 (1983).)

Larkin, J. H. (1981) Enriching Formal Knowledge: A Model for Learning to Solve Textbook Problems. In J. R. Anderson (Ed.), *Cognitive Skills and Their Acquisition*. Hillsdale, NJ: Erlbaum.

Larkin, J. H. (1983) The Role of Problem Representation in Physics. In D. Gentner and A. L. Stevens, *Mental Models*. Hillsdale, NJ: Erlbaum.

Larkin, J. H., McDermott, J., Simon, D. P. and Simon, H. A. (1980) Expert and Novice Performance in Solving Physics Problems. *Science*, **208**, 1335–1342.

Leith, P. (1983) Hierarchically Structured Production Rules. *Computer Journal*, *26*, 1–5.

Lesgold, A. M. (1984) Acquiring Expertise. In J. R. Anderson and S. M. Kosslyn (Eds.), *Tutorials in Learning and Memory*. New York: Freeman.

Lewis, C. (1981) Skill in Algebra. In J. R. Anderson (Ed.), *Cognitive Skills and Their Acquisition*. Hilsdale, NJ: Erlbaum.

Marr, D. (1982) *Vision*. San Francisco: Freeman.

McCelland, J. L. and Rumelhart, D. E. (1981) An Interactive Model of Contextual Effects in Letter Perception: Pt 1, An Account of Basic Findings. *Psychological Review*, **88**, 375–407.

McDermott, J. (1982) R1: A Rule-Based Configurer of Computer Systems. *Artificial Intelligence*, *19*, 39–88.

McKeithen, K. B., Reitman, J. S., Rueter, H. H. and Hirtle, S. C. (1981) Knowledge Organization and Skill Differences in Computer Programmers, *Cognitive Psychology*, **13**, 307–325.

Michalski, R. S. and Chilausky, R. L. (1980) Knowledge Acquisition by Encoding Expert Rules Versus Computer by Induction from Examples: A Case Study Involving Soybean Pathology, *International Journal of Man–Machine Studies*, **12**, 63–87.

Michie, D. (1980) Expert Systems. *Computer Journal*, **23**, 369–376.

Michie, D. (1982) The State of the Art in Machine Learning. In D. Michie (Ed.), *Introductory Readings in Expert Systems*, London: Gordon and Breach.

Miller, G. A. (1956) The Magical Number Seven, Plus or Minus Two: Some Limits on Our Capacity to Process Information. *Psychological Review*, **63**, 81–97.

Miller, P. L. (1984) *A Critiquing Approach to Expert Computer Advice: ATTENDING*. Boston: Pitman.

Minsky, M. (1975) A Framework for Representing Knowledge, In P. H. Winston (Ed.), *The Psychology of Computer Vision*. New York: McGraw-Hill.

Murphy, G. L. and Medin, D. L. (1985) The Role of Theories in Conceptual Coherence. *Psychological Review*, **92**, 289–316.

Murphy, G. L. and Wright, J. C. (1984) Changes in Conceptual Structure with Expertise: Differences Between Real-World Experts and Novices. *Journal of Experimental Psychology: Learning, Memory and Cognition*, **10**, 144–155.

Myers, C. D., Fox, J., Pegram, S. M. and Greaves, M. G. (1983) Knowledge Acquisition for Expert Systems: Experience Using EMYCIN for Leukaemia Diagnosis. In J. Fox (Ed.), *Expert Systems 83*, Churchill College, Cambridge.

Neisser, U. (1976) *Cognitive Psychology*. New York: Appleton.

Newell, A. (1973) Production Systems: Models of Control Structures. In W. G. Chase (Ed.), *Visual Information Processing*. New York: Academic Press.

Newell, A. and Rosenbloom, P. S. (1981) Mechanisms of Skill Acquisition and the Law of Practice. In J. R. Anderson (Ed.), *Cognitive Skills and their Acquisition*. Hillsdale, NJ: Erlbaum.

Newell, A. and Simon, H. A. (1972) *Human Problem Solving*. Englewood Cliffs, NJ: Prentice-Hall.

Newell, A. and Simon, H. A. (1976) Computer Science as Empirical Enquiry: Symbols and Search. (1975 ACM Turing Lecture) *Communications of the ACM*, **19**(3), 113–126.

Nisbett, R. E., Krantz, D. H., Jepson, C. and Kunda, Z. (1983) The Use of Statistical Heuristics in Everyday Inductive Reasoning. *Psychological Review*, **90**, 339–363.

Nisbett, R. E. and Wilson, T. D. (1977) Telling More Than We Can Know: Verbal Reports on Mental Processes. *Psychological Review*, **84**, 231–259.

Norman, D. A. (1981) Twelve Issues for Cognitive Science. In D. A. Norman (Ed.), *Perspectives on Cognitive Science*. Hillsdale, NJ: Erlbaum.

Norman, D. A. (1983) Some Observations on Mental Models. In D. Gentner and A. L. Stevens (Eds.), *Mental Models*. Hillsdale, NJ: Erlbaum.

Pask, G. (1975) *Conversation, Cognition and Learning*. Amsterdam: Elsevier.

Patel, V. L. and Groen, G. J. (1986) Knowledge Based Solution Strategies in Medical Reasoning. *Cognitive Science*, **10**, 91–116.

Paterson, A., Sachs, P. and Turner, M. (1985) ESCORT: The

Application of Causal Knowledge to Real-time Process Control. In M. Merry (Ed.), *Expert Systems 85.* Cambridge: Cambridge University Press.

Pauker, S., Gorry, G., Kassirer, J. and Schwartz, W. (1976) Towards the Simulation of Clinical Cognition. *American Journal of Medicine*, **60**, 981–996.

Pinker, S. (1984) Visual Cognition: An Introduction. *Cognition*, **18**, 1–63.

Pople, H. E. (1982) Heuristic Methods for Imposing Structure on Ill-structured Problems: The Structuring of Medical Diagnostics. In P. Szolovits (Ed.), *Artificial Intelligence in Medicine.* Boulder, Co: Westview.

Popper, K. R. (1963) *Conjectures and Refutations,* London: Routledge.

Posner, M. I. and Keele, W. W. (1970) Retention of Abstract Ideas. *Journal of Experimental Psychology*, **83**, 304–308.

Rayner, E. H. (1958) A Study of Evaluative Problem Solving. Part 1. Observations on Adults. *Quarterly Journal of Experimental Psychology*, **10**, 155–165.

Reder, L. M. and Anderson, J. R. (1980) A Partial Resolution of the Paradox of Interference: The Role of Integrating Knowledge. *Cognitive Psychology*, **12**, 447–472.

Reder, L. M. and Ross, B. H. (1983) Integrated Knowledge in Different Tasks: Positive and Negative Fan Effects. *Journal of Experimental Psychology: Human Learning and Memory*, **8**, 55–72.

Reed, S. K. (1972) Pattern Recognition and Categorization. *Cognitive Psychology*, **3**, 382–407.

Reggia, J. A., Nau, D. S. and Wang, P. Y. (1984) Diagnostic Expert Systems Based on a Set Covering Model. In M. J. Coombs (Ed.), *Developments in Expert Systems.* London: Academic Press. (Also in *International Journal of Man–Machine Studies*, **19**, 437–460 (1983).)

Rich, E. (1983) *Artificial Intelligence.* New York: McGraw-Hill.

Riesbeck, C. K. (1984) Knowledge Reorganization and Reasoning Style. In M. J. Coombs (Ed.), *Developments in Expert Systems.* London: Academic Press.

Rosch, E. (1977) Classification of Real-World Objects: Origins and Representations in Cognition. In P. N. Johnson-Laird and P. C. Wason (Eds.), *Thinking: Readings in Cognitive Science.* Cambridge: Cambridge University Press.

Rosch, E., Mervis, C. B., Gray, W. D., Johnson, D. M. and Boyes-Braem, P. (1976) Basic Objects in Natural Categories. *Cognitive Psychology*, **8**, 382–439.

Rumelhart, D. E., McClelland, J. L. and the PDP Group (1986) *Parallel Distributed Processing: Explorations in the Microstructure of Cognition* (2 volumes). Cambridge, MA: MIT Press.

Rumelhart, D. E. and Norman, D. A. (1978) Accretion, Tuning and Restructuring: Three Modes of Learning. In J. W. Cotton and R. Klatsky (Eds.), *Semantic Factors in Cognition.* Hillsdale, NJ: Erlbaum.

Rumelhart, D. E. and Norman, D. A. (1981) Analogical Processes in Learning. In J. R. Anderson (Ed.), *Cognitive Skills and Their Acquisition.* Hillsdale, NJ: Erlbaum.

Rumelhart, D. E. and Norman, D. A. (1983) *Representation in Memory.* CHIP Technical Report (No. 116). San Diego: Center for Human Information Processing, University of California. (Extracted in A. M. Aitkenhead and J. M. Slack (Eds.), *Issues in Cognitive Modelling.* Hillsdale, NJ: Erlbaum (1985).)

Schank, R. C. (1982) *Dynamic Memory: A Theory of Reminding and Learning in Computers and People.* Cambridge: Cambridge University Press.

Schank, R. C. and Abelson, R. (1977) *Scripts, Plans, Goals and Understanding.* Hillsdale, NJ: Erlbaum.

Schank, R. C. and Slade, S. (1984) Advisory Systems. In W. Reitman (Ed.), *Artificial Intelligence Applications in Business.* Norwood, NJ: Ablex.

Searle, J. (1984) *Brains, Minds and Science.* Reith Lectures, BBC Publications.

Shaw, M. L. G. and Gaines, B. R. (1983) A Computer Aid to Knowledge Engineering. In J. Fox (Ed.), *Expert Systems 83*, Churchill College, Cambridge.

Shiffrin, R. M. and Schneider, W. (1977) Controlled and Automatic Human Information Processing: II. Perceptual Learning, Automatic Attending and a General Theory. *Psychological Review*, **84**, 127–190.

Shortliffe, E. H. (1976) *Computer-Based Medical Consultations: MYCIN.* New York: American Elsevier.

Simon, H. A. (1979) Information-Processing Theory of Human Problem Solving. In W. Estes (Ed.), *Handbook of Learning and Cognitive Processes*, Vol. 5. Hillsdale, NJ: Erlbaum.

Simon, H. A. and Gilmartin, K. (1973) A Simulation of Memory for Chess Positions. *Cognitive Psychology*, **5**, 29–46.

Simons G. L. (1983) *Towards Fifth-Generation Computers.* Manchester: NCC Publications.

Slack, J. M. (1984) Cognitive Science Research. In T. O'Shea and M.

Eisenstadt (Eds.), *Artificial Intelligence: Tools, Techniques, and Applications*. New York: Harper and Row.

Slatter, P. E. (1985) Cognitive Emulation in Expert System Design. *Knowledge Engineering Review*, **1**(2), 28–40.

Slatter, P. E. (1986) Expert Behaviour and Cognition as a Framework for Explanation in Expert Systems. Paper given at the *Alvey Workshop on Explanation*, University of Surrey, Guildford (March).

Sleeman, D. H. (1984) *UMFE: A User Modelling Front End Subsystem*. Heuristic Programming Project, Standford University. Report HPP–84–12.

Sleeman, D. and Brown, J. (Eds.) (1982) *Intelligent Tutoring Systems*. London: Academic Press.

Sloman, A. (1984) Why We Need Many Knowledge Representation Formalisms. In M. A. Bramer (Ed.), *Research and Development in Expert Systems*. Cambridge: Cambrdige University Press.

Smith, E. E., Adams, N. and Schorr, D. (1978) Fact Retrieval and the Paradox of Interference. *Cognitive Psychology*, **10**, 438–464.

Sowa, J. F. (1984) *Conceptual Structures: Information Processing in Mind and Machine*. Reading, MA: Addison-Wesley.

Sparck Jones, K. (1984) Natural Language Interfaces for Expert System.In M. A. Bramer (Ed.), *Research and Development in Expert Systems*. Cambridge: Cambridge University Press.

Sparck Jones, K. (1985) Issues in User Modelling for Expert Systems. In *Proceedings of AISB85*. University of Warwick (April).

Spiegelhalter, D. J. and Knill-Jones, R. P. (1984) Statistical and Knowledge-based Approaches to Clinical Decision-support Systems, with an Application in Gastroenterology. *Journal of the Royal Statistical Society*, **147**(1), 35–77.

Stefik, M., Aikins J., Balzer, R., Benoit, J., Birnbaum, L., Hayes-Roth, F. and Sacerdoti, E. (1982) The Organization of Expert Systems, A Tutorial. *Artificial Intelligence*, **18**, 135–173.

Sternberg, R. J. (1984) Facets of Human Intelligence. In J. R. Anderson and S. M. Kosslyn (Eds.), *Tutorials in Learning and Memory*. New York: Freeman.

Szolovits, P. and Pauker, S. G. (1978) Categorical and Probabilistic Reasoning in Medical Diagnosis. *Artificial Intelligence*, **11**, 115–144.

Tversky, A. and Kahneman, D. (1983) Extensional Versus Intuitive Reasoning: The Conjunction Fallacy in Probability Judgement. *Psychological Review*, **90**, 293–315.

Wallis, J. W. and Shortliffe, E. H. (1982) Explanatory Power for Medical Expert Systems: Studies in the Representation of Causal Relationships for Clinical Consultations. *Methods of Information in Medicine*, **21**, 127–136.

Wason, P. C. and Evans, J. St B. T. (1975) Dual Processes in Reasoning? *Cognition*, **3**, 141–154.

Weizenbaum, J. (1976) *Computer Power and Human Reason: From Judgement to Calculation.* San Francisco: Freeman.

Welbank, M. (1983) *A Review of Knowledge Acquisition Techniques for Expert Systems.* Martlesham Consultancy Services, British Telecom Research Labs: Martlesham Heath, Ipswich.

White, A. P. (1984) Inference Deficiencies in Rule-based Expert systems. In M. A. Bramer (Ed.), *Research and Developments in Expert Systems.* Cambridge: Cambridge University Press.

Whitfield, T. W. A. and Slatter, P. E. (1978) The Evaluation of Architectural Interior Colour as a Function of Style of Furnishings: Categorization Effects. *Scandinavian Journal of Psychology*, **19**, 251–255.

Whitfield, T. W. A. and Slatter, P. E. (1979) The Effects of Categorisation and Prototypicality on Aesthetic Choice in a Furniture Selection Task. *British Journal of Psychology*, **70**, 65–75.

Wielinga, B. J. and Breuker, J. A. (1984) *Interpretation of Verbal Data for Knowledge Acquisition.* Report 1.4, Esprit Project 12, University of Amsterdam.

Wielinga, B. J. and Breuker, J. A. (1986) Models of Expertise. *Proceedings of ECAI'86*, **1**, 306–318.

Wilkins, D. C., Buchanan, B. G. and Clancey, W. J. (1984) *Inferring an Expert's Reasoning by Watching.* Heuristic Programming Project, Stanford University. Report HPP-84-29.

Williams, M. D., Hollan, J. D. and Stevens, A. L. (1983) Human Reasoning about a Simple Physical System. In D. Gentner and A. L. Stevens (Eds.), *Mental Models.* Hillsdale, NJ: Erlbaum.

Winograd, T. (1975) Frame Representations and the Declarative/Procedural Controversy. In D. G. Bobrow and A. Collins (Eds.), *Representation and Understanding: Studies in Cognitive Science.* New York: Academic Press.

Woods, D. D. (1986) Cognitive Technologies: The Design of Joint Human–Machine Cognitive Systems. *AI Magazine*, **6**(4), 86–92.

Young, R. M. (1979) Production Systems for Modelling Human Cognition. In D. Michie (Ed.), *Expert Systems in The Micro-Electronic Age.* Edinburgh: Edinburgh University Press.

Young, R. M. (1981) The Machine Inside the Machine: Users' Models of Pocket Calculators. *International Journal of Man- -Machine Studies*, **15**, 51–85.

Young, R. M. (1985) Human Interface Aspects of Expert Systems. In J. Fox (Ed.), *State of the Art Report in Expert Systems*. Pergamon Infotech.

Young, R. M. and O'Shea, T. (1981) Errors in Children's Subtraction. *Cognitive Science*, **5**, 153–177.

Zimmer, A. C. (1984) A Model for the Interpretation of Verbal Predictions. In M. J. Coombs (Ed.), *Developments in Expert Systems*. London: Academic Press.

Author index

Subject index

abstract coding, 40, 42
abstraction, 26, 45
acceptance criteria, 89
accretion, 25
ACRONYM, 99
activation, 54, 74
ACT*, 45, 97
AI techniques, 9, 61, 73, 78, 85, 86, 89, 91, 98, 111
algebra, 23, 39, 40
algorithms, 49, 102, 107, 123
analogical representations, 53, 58, 97, 121, 123
analogical transfer, 40
analogy, 40, 53
analytic task, 60, 112
arithmetic, 29, 48, 53, 89
artificial intelligence (AI), 7, 9, 10, 13, 17, 39, 44, 49, 54, 59, 63, 73, 86, 90, 94, 106, 121
artificial systems, 13, 27, 52, 118
ATTENDING, 84
automated processes, 31, 32, 41, 117
automization, 31–33, 39
availability, 36, 37, 58, 104

backtracking, 74
backward reasoning 34, 35, 57, 58, 69, 97, 102, 123
Bayes' Theorem, 36, 38, 57, 103, 104, 121
behavioural mimicry, 73, 74, 76
Behaviourism, 18
blackboard architecture, 50, 76, 97, 98, 99
boardgames, 23
Boolean representations, 57, 58
breadth-first strategy, 35, 121
BUGGY, 90

categorization, 26, 40
causal models, 27, 58
chess, 23–25, 28, 30, 31, 38, 39

chunking, 28, 32, 38, 39, 42, 49, 58, 99, 102, 110
classificatory knowledge, 72
clinical, 11, 23, 35, 38, 43, 73, 74–76, 83, 87, 100, 104, 112
COBOL, 101
cognitive architecture, 9, 24, 93, 94, 96–98
cognitive coupling, 47
cognitive functions, 47, 79, 83, 84, 87, 98, 118, 121
cognitive modelling, 7, 10, 21, 46, 96, 97, 106, 117
cognitive overload, 21, 34, 100
cognitive processor, 24, 94–96
cognitive psychology, 7, 8, 9, 10, 11, 14, 16–19, 31, 34, 43, 47, 53, 54, 59, 68, 70, 76, 80, 83, 93, 94, 98, 101, 106, 118, 122
cognitive science, 13, 20–22, 59, 62, 86, 93, 98, 117
cognitive weakness, 48, 50
combinatorial explosion, 49, 60
competence, 17, 75, 83, 89
competent expert systems, 83, 103
compiled knowledge, 29, 99, 103, 110
completeness, 56, 67
composite productions, 29, 42
computational models, 9, 13, 59, 62
computational power, 46, 97
computer programming, 23, 35, 39, 40
concepts, 26, 27, 40, 42, 46, 58, 70–72, 76, 77, 80–82, 85, 89, 90, 98, 110, 112
Conceptual Learning System, 46
conceptual sorting, 23, 71, 72, 120
configurations, 26, 38, 58
connectionism, 106–109, 111
constraints, 15, 52, 56, 59, 84, 86, 117, 118
control, 46, 57, 58, 64, 65, 74, 84, 87, 96, 97, 100
controlled processes, 31
Conversation Theory, 85
co-operative problem solving, 84, 113, 119
correctness, 56, 57, 60
crisp concepts, 26
critiquing, 79, 84, 85–87, 121